NO LONG
SEATTL

D0175116

# GROWING UP WITH
# A SINGLE PARENT

What Hurts, What Helps

# GROWING UP WITH A SINGLE PARENT

What Hurts,
What Helps

Sara McLanahan
Gary Sandefur

**HARVARD UNIVERSITY PRESS**
Cambridge, Massachusetts
London, England

Copyright © 1994 by the President and Fellows of Harvard College
All rights reserved
Printed in the United States of America
Second printing, 1996

*Library of Congress Cataloging-in-Publication Data*

McLanahan, Sara.
Growing up with a single parent : what hurts, what helps /
Sara McLanahan, Gary Sandefur
p.   cm.
Includes bibliographical references and index.
ISBN 0-674-36407-4 (cloth)
ISBN 0-674-36408-2 (pbk.)
1. Children of single parents—United States. 2. Single-parent
family—United States. I. Sandefur, Gary D., 1951–  . II. Title.
HQ777.4.M39      1994
306.85'6—dc20
94-19995
CIP

For Sara, Jay, and
Anna McLanahan,
Leah and Lynn Garfinkel,
Becky and Carol Sandefur

# Acknowledgments

Many people have provided intellectual guidance and encouragement during the ten years that we have been studying the consequences of single parenthood. Our colleagues Nan Astone, Larry Bumpass, Lynne Casper, Michael Foster, Irwin Garfinkel, Thomas Hanson, Charles Manski, Nadine Marks, Daniel Powers, Judith Seltzer, Elizabeth Thomson, and Roger Wojtkiewicz collaborated with us on numerous papers, and their contributions are evident throughout this book.

The Institute for Research on Poverty at the University of Wisconsin has been our primary intellectual home. Robert Lampman organized the seminar on the underclass that prompted us to begin our work on single motherhood. Sheldon Danziger masterminded our initial collaboration and has been a constant source of encouragement. Irwin Garfinkel taught us about child support reform. And Charles Manski helped us with many of the thornier statistical problems. Sandra Danziger, Robert Haveman, and Barbara Wolfe shared our interests in child poverty and provided intellectual stimulation.

Several colleagues took the time to read and comment on earlier drafts of the manuscript—Andrew Cherlin, Sheldon Danziger, Frank Furstenberg Jr., Irwin Garfinkel, Peter Gottschalk, Christopher Jencks, Philip Morgan, and Judith Seltzer. Their advice was invaluable, and much of it is reflected in the final version of the book. At Harvard University Press, Michael Aronson, our editor, pushed us to say more about social capital, and Susan Wallace Boehmer helped flesh out the story and insisted that we treat nonresident fathers fairly. Over the years Steve Cook, James Hsueh, Mei-chen Hu, Juliet King, Karen Kurz, Brian Martinson, Kelly Raley, and Maureen Waller provided excellent research assistance. Terence Kelly typed numerous versions of the manuscript and, along with Paul Dudenhefer, proofread the final draft. We are grateful to all of these people for their contributions.

The National Institute of Child Health and Human Development provided financial support (R01-HD19375), and Jeffrey Evans, our project officer, helped us survive the budget cuts. We thank him for his enthusiasm and support. Sara McLanahan spent a semester as a visiting scholar at the Russell Sage Foundation in 1989, where she began writing a draft of the book. The Ford Foundation, the Foundation for Child Development, and the Graduate School of the University of Wisconsin also provided financial support on numerous occasions over the past ten years.

Finally, we owe a special intellectual debt to James Coleman for his work on social capital, to William J. Wilson for teaching us about the importance of neighborhoods and community cohesion, and to Irwin Garfinkel for developing a Child Support Assurance System and for helping us understand the value of universal policies.

# Contents

# GROWING UP WITH
# A SINGLE PARENT

What Hurts, What Helps

# CHAPTER ONE

# WHY WE CARE ABOUT SINGLE PARENTHOOD

In the summer of 1992, the Vice President of the United States, Dan Quayle, condemned Murphy Brown—the lead character in a popular television show—for giving birth out of wedlock. In doing so he focused national attention on single mothers and reopened an old debate over the consequences of family structure for children and for the nation as a whole. The public reaction was intense and sharply divided. Some people argued that single motherhood had no known long-term negative consequences for children. Others claimed it was the major cause of child poverty, delinquency, and high school failure. And still others argued that even if single motherhood were harmful in some way, we should not say so for fear of stigmatizing single mothers and their children.[1]

We disagree with all three positions. First, we reject the claim that children raised by only one parent do just as well as children raised by both parents. We have been studying this question for ten years, and in our opinion the evidence is quite clear: *Children who grow up in a household with only one biological parent are worse off, on average, than children who grow up in a household with both of their biological parents, regardless of the parents' race or educational background, regardless of whether the parents are married when the child is born, and regardless of whether the resident parent remarries.* Compared with teenagers of similar background who grow up with both parents at home, adolescents who have lived apart from one of their parents during some period of childhood are twice as likely to drop out of high school, twice as likely to have a child before age twenty, and one and a half times as likely to be "idle"—out of school and out of work—in their late teens and early twenties.

But are single motherhood and father absence therefore the root cause of child poverty, school failure, and juvenile delinquency? Our findings lead us to say no. While living with just one parent increases the risk of each of these negative outcomes, it is not the only, or even the major, cause of them. Growing up with a single parent is just one among many factors that put children at risk of failure, just as lack of exercise is only one among many factors that put people at risk for heart disease. Many people who *don't* exercise never suffer a heart attack, and many children raised by single mothers grow up to be quite successful.

One way to assess the impact of family structure on a problem such as high school failure is to compare the dropout rate of all children with the dropout rate of children in two-parent families that have suffered no disruption. During the 1980s, the dropout rate was about 19 percent overall and about 13 percent for children who lived with both their parents.[2] So even if there were no family disruption, the high school dropout rate would still be at least 13 percent. Clearly, most school failure is being caused by something other than single motherhood. But just as clearly, children with an absent parent are at significantly greater risk than their peers who have two biological parents at home.

Finally, we reject the argument that people should not talk about the negative consequences of single motherhood for fear of stigmatizing single mothers and their children. While we appreciate the compassion that lies behind this position, we disagree with the bottom line. Indeed, we believe that *not* talking about these problems does more harm than good. Nearly a third of infants born today are children of unmarried mothers. Of the children born to married parents, about 45 percent are expected to experience their parents' divorce before reaching age eighteen.[3] In other words, well over half of the children born in 1992 will spend all or some of their childhood apart from one of their parents. If we want to develop policies to help these children, and if we want to persuade citizens that government should try to help, we must begin by acknowledging that a substantial proportion of our nation's youth is at risk.

While talking about the downside of single motherhood may make some adults (and children) feel worse off in the short run, it may make everyone better off in the long run. At a minimum, parents need to be informed about the possible consequences to their children of a decision to live apart. (No one would argue that information on the potential benefits of exercise should be withheld because it stigmatizes couch potatoes.)

In this book, we argue that growing up with only one biological parent frequently deprives children of important economic, parental, and community resources, and that these deprivations ultimately undermine their chances of future success. Low income—and the sudden drop in income that often is associated with divorce—is the most important factor in children's lower achievement in single-parent homes, accounting for about half of the disadvantage. Inadequate parental guidance and attention and the lack of ties to community resources account for most of the remaining disadvantage.

We view the lack of parental and community resources as a deficit in what the sociologist James Coleman calls *social capital*.[4] Social capital is an asset that is created and maintained by relationships of commitment and trust. It functions as a conduit of information as well as a source of emotional and economic support, and it can be just as important as financial capital in promoting children's future success. The decision of parents to live apart—whether as a result of divorce or an initial decision not to marry—damages, and sometimes destroys, the social capital that might have been available to the child had the parents lived together.

It does this, first and most importantly, by weakening the connection between the child and the father. When a father lives in a separate household, he is usually less committed to his child and less trusting of the child's mother. Hence he is less willing to invest time and money in the child's welfare. A weakened father-child relationship can also undermine a child's trust in both parents and increase his uncertainty about the future, making him more difficult to manage. And finally, family disruption may reduce a child's access to social capital outside the family by weakening connections to other adults and institutions in the community that would have been available to the child had the relationship with the father remained intact. This can happen because the father moves out of town, breaking the link between the child and the father's network of friends and associates, or because the mother and child move to a new neighborhood or city, breaking the child's connections not just with the father but with teachers, friends, and neighbors.

We base our conclusions on evidence taken from four nationally representative data sets, including three longitudinal surveys and a fourth survey with retrospective data on children's living arrangements growing up. (Each of these data sets, including the major variables, is described in detail in Appendix A.) We examine a wide variety of child outcomes, including high school grades and graduation, college attendance and graduation, early childbearing and marriage, and early labor force attachment. While this set of outcomes does not cover all aspects of well-being, we believe it is a good indicator of a child's chances of economic success in adulthood, defined as being able to support oneself at a standard of living above the poverty line and being able to maintain a steady income throughout the year and from one year to the next. While economic independence and security are not the only measures of success, in a market-oriented economy such as ours they are fundamental. Without some degree of economic independence, a person is unlikely to achieve high self-esteem or a sense of control over her life (psychological success). Nor is she likely to command the respect of her peers (social success). Financial dependence and insecurity also make it harder to achieve family stability and community cohesion, other indicators of social success.

Since many of the outcomes we focus on in this book are relatively rare among children from advantaged backgrounds, middle-class parents may question whether a study of such events is relevant to their child's situation. We believe it is, for several reasons. First, some of our indicators, such as high school grade-point average and college performance, are directly relevant to middle-class parents' concerns. Second, while the chance that a middle-class child will drop out of high school or become a teen mother is very low, it is higher than the likelihood that he or she will be severely injured or killed in a car accident. Yet parents take the latter very seriously. And finally, we believe that much can be learned from studying the factors that buffer children from the negative consequences of rare events. These same factors are likely to be important buffers in other areas of children's lives, and presumably middle-class parents want to know about them.

For example, our study shows that income loss and residential mobility may be just as damaging for children as low income and living in a poor neighborhood. This suggests that, in the event of a divorce, middle-class parents should make an effort to ensure a stable income for their child and should minimize the number of times the child changes schools or neighborhoods. They should do this not to lower the risk that their teenage daughter might become pregnant or drop out of high school (unlikely events in divorced middle-class families) but to lower the risk that her grade-point average and interest in a college education will decline.

In most of our analyses, our family classification scheme is based on two criteria: (1) whether or not a child was living with both biological parents at age sixteen; and, if not, (2) whether the custodial parent was married or not. We treat all families with two biological parents alike, even though we recognize that some parents are psychologically "absent" despite living in the same household as their child, and that some separated or divorced parents are very close to their children although they are living in a different household. Children who were living with only one of their biological parents at age sixteen are classified as living in either a "single-parent family" or a "stepfamily," depending on whether the resident parent was single or remarried. Single parents may be divorced, separated, never married, or widowed.

We reserve the term "two-parent family" for children who were living with both biological parents at age sixteen. While stepfamilies are often classified as two-parent families in some studies, we believe this is a serious distortion of the families' experiences. Nearly all children in stepfamilies have lived in a single-parent family at one time, and nearly all of them have *more than* two parents now. Some have as many as four or five parents, depending on how often their biological parents have married.

We frequently use the term "disrupted family" to characterize children whose biological parents live apart. All children with a nonresident parent share a common experience insofar as their parents' relationship, *from the child's point of view*, is "disrupted," even for those children who have never lived with both parents. We occasionally use the term "one-parent family" to describe children who were living with only one biological parent at age sixteen. A one-parent family may be either a single-parent family or a stepfamily, depending on the context.

We do not attempt to distinguish between children born outside marriage and those born within marriage in most of our analyses of disrupted families. This distinction has become increasingly blurred over time, as divorce and cohabitation have become more common. Nearly a third of children born outside marriage are born to divorced or separated mothers, and over a quarter are born to cohabiting couples, a majority of whom eventually marry.[5] We believe these two sets of children are similar in many ways, and we will provide evidence to support this claim.

Some single-parent families are headed by fathers, but the vast majority are headed by women. Therefore when we use the term "single parent," we are referring to the biological mother rather than father, unless the context suggests otherwise. Since most stepparents are men, we use the terms "stepfather" and "stepparent" interchangeably. The term "nonresident father" refers to a biological father who does not live in a household with his child.

Joint custody arrangements, while not common, are found in many communities, particularly in more privileged socioeconomic groups. In most such families, only one parent has physical (as opposed to legal) custody of the child, and therefore the child is living in a single-parent family, according to our definition. Even in cases where the parents share physical as well as legal custody, the child is not living with both parents *at the same time*. In our opinion, this is the critical point. Whether or not high levels of contact with both biological parents can reduce or eliminate the negative consequences associated with divorce is an open question. To date, researchers have found very little evidence that it does.[6] Of course joint custody is a relatively new phenomenon, and it is too soon to tell how this arrangement will affect children's well-being in the long run.

Before examining the evidence for the effects of family structure on children's future success, we would like to address here an important preliminary question.

## WHY IS SINGLE MOTHERHOOD SO CONTROVERSIAL?

The controversies surrounding single motherhood are both political and scientific. To get an idea of the politics underlying the debate over single mothers, consider the Moynihan Report of nearly thirty years ago. In the summer of 1965, Daniel P. Moynihan, then Assistant Secretary of Labor and now Senator from New York, issued a report on the African American family. The report concluded that single motherhood was a growing problem in poor urban communities, and that if left unchecked it could undermine much of the progress that had been achieved in the early 1960s by the civil rights movement. Moynihan blamed the increasing number of female-headed families principally on rising male unemployment, and he called on the federal government to play a more active role in ensuring jobs for black men.[7] However, because he warned that single motherhood was taking on a life of its own among the urban poor, the report was roundly criticized by black leaders as well as white liberals, and Moynihan and his colleagues were accused of "blaming the victim" for problems beyond their control.[8]

The controversy surrounding the Moynihan Report is instructive insofar as it shows that concern for single mothers can easily be interpreted as condemnation of poor black mothers. Why would this be so? Why would pointing out that a group of people has problems be seen as an attack on that group?

The explanation lies in the fact that single motherhood is an *achieved* rather than an *ascribed* status. An ascribed status is something a person is born with, like race or sex. An achieved status is something a person earns for himself or herself, like years of schooling or occupation. People choose whether or not to marry and whether or not to have a child, and therefore they bear some responsibility for the consequences of their decisions. By linking African American poverty to changes in family structure, the Moynihan Report seemed to be saying that black men and women were somehow responsible for their poor economic condition. This so-called "blaming the victim" did not sit well with those who believed that racism and lack of opportunity were the principal causes of black poverty in the early 1960s.

Even today, many people view the term "single mother" as a codeword for "black, welfare mother." And they continue to view the debate over single motherhood as a debate over whether high poverty rates in the black community are due to lack of opportunity or to choices about marriage and childbearing made by black women and men.[9] Thus, it is not surprising that discussions of single motherhood precipitate strong reactions in many parts of the country.

More recently, single motherhood has come to be associated with women's independence and gender equality. The fact that Vice President Quayle chose Murphy Brown, a white professional woman, as the focus of his remarks makes this link quite explicit. In this case the issue is not so much whether single motherhood is an achieved or ascribed status; the issue is whether women have the right, in a moral sense, to pursue careers, to live independently from men, and to raise children on their own. For many advocates of women's rights, the answer to each of these questions is clearly yes. They view public concern over single motherhood as an attempt to force women back into the traditional roles of housewife and homemaker "for the sake of their children."

But the politics of race and gender is not the only reason single motherhood is controversial. Even social scientists do not always agree about the facts. This was true at the time of the Moynihan Report, and it continues to be true today, despite thirty years of additional research on the subject. Disagreements arise in part because analysts are addressing different questions. They also arise because analysts disagree about the answer to the same question.

With respect to the first point, there are at least three questions that might be asked about the consequences of single motherhood. One is: Are children who grow up with only one biological parent less successful in adulthood, on average, than children who grow up with both parents? Another is: Are children with an absent parent less successful than children from two-parent families with similar known characteristics, such as race or parents' income and education? And finally, one might ask: Would children who grow up with only one parent have done better if their parents had stayed together?

The first question is easy, and social scientists agree about the facts in this case. Children who live with both parents do better, on average, than children who live with only one parent or with neither parent. If we compare the high school graduation rates of the children in one of our samples, for example, we find that 87 percent of children from two-parent families receive a high school degree by age twenty, as compared with 68 percent of children from families with only one biological parent.[10] Most reasonable people would agree that a gap of 19 percentage points is a large and important difference.

Knowing that such a difference exists does not tell us very much, however. Many reasons other than family structure could explain why children from single-parent families and stepfamilies might do less well in school than children from two-parent families. For example, children who live with only one biological parent are less likely to have college-educated parents than children from two-parent families, and they are more likely to be black or Hispanic and therefore subject to racial discrimination or language barriers. Unless we take these other factors into account, we cannot say how much of the difference in school achievement is due to family structure and how much is due to some other characteristic such as race or parents' education.

When we compare children with similar racial and educational backgrounds, the gap in high school graduation rates between children of one-parent and two-parent families falls from 19 percentage points to 16 points. If we also adjust for differences in place of residence, for the number of children in the family, and for the parents' occupational status, the gap falls to 15 percentage points. Thus, the answer to the question of whether family structure affects children with similar known characteristics is yes.

Notice that in the previous examples we did not compare children with similar family incomes. This is because we view low income as partly the *result*, as well as partly the cause, of family disruption. In our model of how the process works, we see separation and divorce as leading to a loss of income, which in turn leads to children's lower success in school. Even in the case of children born to unmarried parents, the parents' decision to live apart represents a loss of *future* income for the child. Had the parents chosen to live together and pool their incomes, the child's standard of living would have been higher. If we want to measure the *total* effect of family disruption on children, it would be inappropriate to compare children with similar income levels. Doing so would lead us to underestimate the consequences of single parenthood. Ultimately, we may want to know how much of the effect of family disruption is due to loss of income, but first we must estimate the total effect.

On the other hand, low income is undeniably, to some degree, a cause of family structure. We know that parents who are poor are more likely to divorce, and less likely to marry in the first place, than parents who are well off financially. Therefore, not adjusting for family income prior to divorce (or prior to an out-of-wedlock birth) may lead to an overestimation of the total effect of family disruption on children.

A good deal of the disagreement among researchers over whether or not single parenthood harms children arises over just this issue of how to treat income. Analysts who believe that low income predates single parenthood often argue that family structure per se has no negative consequences for children. By this they mean that family structure does not matter once income is taken into account.

In contrast, analysts who believe that low income is a consequence of divorce and out-of-wedlock birth often argue that living with a single parent has a large negative effect on children, much of which is due to economic deprivation. In Chapter 5, we will show that *declines* in income following divorce, regardless of what the income was to begin with, account for as much as half of the higher risk of dropping out of high school, becoming a teen mother, and being idle for children in single-parent families.

The third question—would children with an absent parent have done better if their parents had stayed together—is the most difficult to answer. And, not surprisingly, it is also the most controversial. To really answer the question, we would need to run an experiment that randomly assigns people to two-parent and one-parent families. Otherwise, we cannot rule out the possibility that some third variable—such as illness in the family or the father's unemployment—is both causing parents to live apart and causing children to do worse in school. Adjusting for known characteristics, such as race and parents' education, reduces the possibility that family structure is serving as a proxy for some other variable, but it does not eliminate the possibility.

We know, for example, that families with an alcoholic or abusive parent or families in which there is a good deal of conflict between the parents are more likely to break up than other families.[11] We also know that the children in such families have a higher risk of school failure. Either of these characteristics—conflict or alcoholism—could, alone, account for the higher dropout rate of children in single-parent families or stepfamilies. Without a randomized experiment, we can never rule out the possibility that some other variable is causing both family structure and children's failure in school. Because of this, analysts will always disagree about whether family structure plays a *causal* role in determining child well-being.[12]

## OUR STRATEGY

In this book we will focus on answering the second question posed above: Do children who grow up with a single mother or a mother and stepfather have worse outcomes than children with similar known characteristics who grow up with both of their biological parents? All of the estimates reported in Chapters 3 through 7 are based on models that adjust for family background differences, including race, mother's education, father's education, number of siblings, and place of residence. Thus, we can be confident that the differences in child well-being that we report are not due to differences in this set of background characteristics.[13]

We will also provide some information on the third question: Would children from divorced families have done better if their parents had stayed together? In Chapters 5 through 7 we report estimates based on models that adjust for predivorce differences in family resources and children's well-being. These models provide a more conservative estimate of the effect of family instability on children.[14] This part of our analysis is limited, however. Most of the indicators of child well-being that we look at closely occur only once—for example, dropping out of high school or having a child out of wedlock. Thus, there is no predisruption measure of child well-being. Obviously, we cannot measure predisruption differences for the large and growing group of children who were born out of wedlock and who have never lived with their fathers.

In addition to adjusting for observed predivorce differences in family resources and children's well-being, we also have used statistical techniques to address the question of how well children *would have done* had their parents stayed together. The results based on these statistical techniques (reported in Appendix B) suggest that the numbers presented in this book come pretty close to answering the third question, even though they are not based on randomized experiments.[15]

## WHY WE NEED ANOTHER BOOK ON
## SINGLE PARENTHOOD

A good deal has been written during the past thirty years about the consequences of single parenthood for children, and the conventional wisdom on the subject has changed several times. Indeed, when we began our research in the early 1980s, the conventional wisdom was that children from single-parent families were no worse off than children from two-parent families. Our investigation was stimulated by a series of articles on the "underclass" by Ken Auletta which first appeared in the *New Yorker* in 1981.[16] Auletta was reporting on a study of the Supported Work Demonstration Project—an education and training program for disadvantaged people. The targeted population, and those labeled underclass by Auletta, included former criminals, drug addicts and substance abusers, long-term unemployed males, and single mothers who had been on welfare for at least six years. What caught our eye was the fact that a large proportion of participants in the program—including the mothers on welfare—had grown up in single-mother families. The implication was that single-mother families were somehow responsible for the growth of an underclass. The idea that single mothers were to blame for producing a class of criminals, drug addicts, jobless men, and long-term welfare recipients seemed wrongheaded, given what we had learned as graduate students in the 1970s. Hadn't social scientists demonstrated that the negative effects attributed to single motherhood were really due to poverty and racial discrimination? So we thought when we began our study.

Initially, our examination of the early research yielded evidence that was consistent with our expectations. During the 1950s and 1960s most studies showing the negative consequences of single parenthood were based on small, convenience samples (children in treatment for psychological disorders or wards of the court) and so could not be generalized to the population. In 1973 this conventional wisdom that children who grow up with single mothers have serious problems was challenged by Elizabeth Herzog and Cecilia Sudia in their lengthy review of the research on single motherhood entitled "Children in Fatherless Families."[17] They criticized the existing studies on a number of methodological grounds and concluded that most of them could not be used to support the argument that single motherhood was bad for children. Herzog and Sudia noted that father absence *did* appear to have some negative consequences for children, but that most of these consequences were *probably* due to differences in socioeconomic status.

The Herzog and Sudia review made it clear that the scientific basis for the concern over single-mother families was weak. However, instead of stimulating a large-scale effort to test the hypothesis that living in a one-parent family had *no* negative consequences for children, once social class differences were taken into account, the review itself was taken as evidence that *no consequences existed*. This occurred despite the fact that Herzog and Sudia carried out no new empirical research and despite their explicit statement that living in a one-parent family had *some* negative consequences for children. In short, the empirical work necessary for testing the effect of family structure on the well-being of children had not been done.[18]

After the controversy over the Moynihan Report, researchers tended to avoid the topic of single motherhood. A few ethnographic studies appeared, but these focused on the strengths of the black family and the ways in which single mothers successfully coped with poverty and stress. The most famous of these was Carol Stack's *All Our Kin,* which described the exchange networks on which single mothers relied for economic and social support.[19] While Stack's study provided us with a strong sense of the day-to-day experiences of single mothers (and while her study is one of the best descriptions we have of the importance of social capital), she did not discuss the children of poor single mothers or compare the children of single mothers with children in two-parent families. Furthermore, while serving as a useful antidote to the grim view that had prevailed in the sixties, the ethnographic studies in the 1970s created a new myth about the extended families and strong support networks available to poor single mothers.

Eventually a line of research emerged that addressed the question of family structure and children's well-being in a way that was less controversial. The new studies were based on longitudinal designs and focused on white middle-class families and on divorce rather than desertion and out-of-wedlock birth. Two of these studies were particularly influential: Judith Wallerstein's research on 60 divorcing couples in the Berkeley, California, area, and Mavis Hetherington's study of 124 families in Virginia.[20] Both researchers found that divorce had negative consequences for children, at least during the initial period after the parents' separation. Since nearly all of the subjects were white and middle class, these studies did not feed negative stereotypes about poor minority families, and they did not arouse the kind of controversy that was stimulated by the Moynihan Report.

The research on divorce culminated in the National Survey of Children, which was carried out in 1976 and again in 1981 and 1987 under the direction of Frank Furstenberg Jr., Nicholas Zill, and their colleagues. These new data provided researchers with a nationally representative sample of approximately 2,000 children which could be used to test many of the ideas suggested by Hetherington and Wallerstein in their work with small, local samples. Overall, the National Survey of Children confirmed the finding that divorce reduces children's school performance and social adjustment.[21]

While these newer studies of white middle-class divorce represent a major advancement in our knowledge of the effects of family instability on children, they do not answer many of the questions that prompted our initial inquiry.

First, these studies of divorce do not tell us about the long-term consequences of growing up in a one-parent family. The children in the Hetherington study have only recently entered adolescence, and most of the evidence we have from the National Survey of Children is based on children in middle childhood and early adolescence.

The Wallerstein and Blakeslee study would appear to be an exception, since the children of the original families were reinterviewed in their early twenties and asked about their current relationships. Indeed, the Wallerstein and Blakeslee book, *Second Chances,* is widely cited as evidence that divorce has lasting negative effects on children.[22] Unfortunately, this study had no control group, and therefore we cannot tell whether the problems these young men and women were experiencing are substantially different from the problems experienced by the average young adult in the 1980s. The fact that the children themselves attribute their difficulties to their parents' divorce is suggestive in this regard but not conclusive.

Second, the divorce research does not tell us about the experiences of children born to unmarried mothers, who represent an increasing proportion of children living with single parents. Demographers now predict that half of all children who will live with single parents in the future will do so because of a nonmarital birth.[23] Clearly, to fully understand the consequences of single parenthood, children born to unmarried mothers must be included in studies of family structure.

Third, the studies of divorce do not give us a good sense of the size of the effect of family structure on child well-being. They simply tell us that a correlation exists and that it is statistically significant. This gives researchers a considerable amount of latitude in interpreting their results, which is one reason there is so much disagreement within the social science community. Some researchers point to the fact that most children who grow up in one-parent families do quite well (the glass is half full), whereas others point to the fact that they do less well, on average, than children in two-parent families (the glass is half empty). Both views are correct, but neither takes us far enough.

Fourth, existing studies do not tell us whether the effects of single parenthood differ by race and class. Again, this is primarily a function of sample design. Whereas at one point in the early sixties the debate over single parenthood was too strongly focused on black families, one might argue that in the seventies and early eighties it was too focused on white middle-class families. There are good theoretical arguments for expecting the effects of single parenthood to be stronger or weaker for different racial and ethnic groups. But in order to examine these questions empirically, we must have data that include blacks and other ethnic minorities as well as whites.

Finally, past research tells us very little about *why* living with only one biological parent affects children negatively, or what might be done to reverse these patterns. These are the most important questions, and the most difficult to answer. Herzog and Sudia's original hypothesis—that many of the disadvantages found among the children of single mothers were due to low socioeconomic status—remained untested, in part because people thought they already knew the answer, and in part because the data needed to test these hypotheses did not exist. Moreover, assuming that some of the difference between children from one-parent and two-parent families is due to differences in family income, we need to know *how much* difference income makes, and how much we could improve children's well-being by simply increasing their family income. Moreover, if income turns out to be the major factor, those single mothers who are financially comfortable, like Murphy Brown, would not have to worry quite so much about having put their children at risk for failure.

In sum, many important questions regarding the effects of single parenthood on children remain unanswered.[24] Are the consequences of single parenthood large enough to merit our concern? Is the experience of single parenthood similar for all racial and ethnic groups and for children born to married and unmarried parents? How much of the difference in children's achievement is due to differences in family income? How much is due to differences in parental and community resources? These are the questions that we attempt to answer in this book.

## ORGANIZATION OF THE BOOK

In Chapter 2 we develop in greater detail our basic theory for why single parenthood reduces children's well-being. Chapter 3 presents the first set of empirical results. Here we compare children living with both parents to children living with only one parent, focusing particularly on educational achievement, labor force attachment, and early childbearing. Chapter 4 looks at children from single-parent families and asks whether factors such as the cause of the family's structure (divorce, desertion, or death), the timing and duration of single motherhood, and the mother's remarriage make a difference for children's future well-being.

Chapters 5 through 7 examine three major explanations for why children in one-parent families do less well than children in two-parent families. Chapter 5 focuses on the role of income in accounting for differences in children's achievement. Chapter 6 considers the role of parenting styles, and the contribution of non-resident fathers as well as stepfathers to the child's social capital. And Chapter 7 asks whether the quality of the communities in which children live and the quality of their ties to the community are major factors in the well-being of children who live with one parent. Chapter 8 summarizes the major findings of our research and discusses their implications for parents, children, and policy-makers.

# CHAPTER TWO

# HOW FATHER ABSENCE LOWERS CHILDREN'S WELL-BEING

How do we measure success in adulthood? Through what processes do parents promote their children's success, and how does family disruption undermine these processes?

In a market economy such as the United States', economic well-being is fundamental to all other forms of well-being. Thus, in our study we focus on economic success—being able to support oneself at a standard of living above the poverty line and being able to maintain a steady income throughout the year and from one year to the next. We believe that psychological success—self-esteem or a sense of control over one's life—is more difficult to achieve and maintain when a person is totally dependent on other people or on the government for his basic needs. We also believe social success, defined as respect from peers and stability in one's family and community relationships, is compromised by economic insecurity and dependence. Thus, while money cannot buy happiness, the lack of money makes it much harder for a person to feel good about himself and to maintain good relationships with other people.

To determine whether a young man or woman is likely to be economically successful, we focus on three areas of achievement: educational attainment, labor force attachment, and early family formation.

*Educational attainment* is one of the best predictors we have of a person's future income. People who finish high school and go on to college—especially those who graduate from college—have a much better chance of achieving financial security during adulthood than individuals who drop out of high school.

High school dropout rates have been going down since 1960, and the proportion of children receiving high school diplomas (or equivalency diplomas) has been going up. While these trends are encouraging, there are several reasons for not taking them for granted. First, the rise in high school graduation rates came to an abrupt halt at the end of the 1970s.[1] Second, the percentage of new graduates receiving equivalency diplomas grew from 5 percent in 1970 to over 14 percent in 1990. Since there is some evidence that a General Equivalency Diploma (GED) is *not* equivalent to a high school diploma in terms of future earnings, the increase in GEDs suggests that education levels actually declined during the 1980s.[2] Most importantly, the cost of *not* finishing high school has also increased, which means that young people with inadequate educations are worse off today than they were twenty years ago. Whereas at one time a person without a high school degree might hope to obtain a secure, well-paying manufacturing job, today such jobs are rapidly disappearing. Moreover, the trend in college education—which is of greater concern to middle-class parents than the trend in high school graduation—has also taken a disturbing turn during the past decade. After increasing steadily during the 1960s and 1970s, the percent of young adults with a college degree leveled off during the 1980s. The picture was even worse for young men. Whereas young women were more likely to have a college degree in 1990 than in 1980, young men were less likely to have completed college. These changes occurred despite the fact that the value of a college degree increased substantially during the 1980s. In 1990 the average young man twenty-five to thirty-four with a college degree earned 62 percent more than the average young man with a high school degree, assuming that both parties worked full time. In 1980 he earned only 33 percent more than the average young man with a high school diploma. The numbers for women were 68 percent and 42 percent.[3]

Another marker of future economic success is *labor force attachment*. After leaving school, young adults must find a job and establish themselves in the labor market. This is not an easy task, and many young people become discouraged if they cannot find work or if their jobs are unrewarding or poorly paid. Sticking to the task and holding down a steady job are good indicators of people's motivation, ability, and skills, and ultimately of their long-term chances of earning a good income.

By the same token, idleness and inactivity are a sign of problems to come.[4] Young adults who are not attached to the labor force or who work only intermittently may not develop the skills necessary for achieving economic security and social success later on. Being idle is also often associated with crime and drug or alcohol abuse.[5]

Since the early 1970s the transition from school to work has become increasingly difficult for many young adults, particularly young black men. In 1970, 9 percent of young black males between the ages of twenty and twenty-four were neither employed nor in school; by 1980 the figure had risen to 27 percent, and by 1990 it was 28 percent. The trend for young white males was in the same direction, although the absolute levels of idleness were much lower. In 1990, 13 percent of young white men were neither working nor in school, up from 9 percent in 1970.[6]

The labor force profile of young women—white and black—is somewhat different from that of young men. Women are more likely than men to be neither working nor in school, although the sex difference has been declining since 1970. The decline in idleness was especially strong among white women, from 41 percent in 1970 to only 26 percent in 1990. Among young black women, the figures were 46 percent and 38 percent respectively.[7]

One reason young women have higher rates of "idleness" or "inactivity" than young men is that they are more likely to be taking care of children. In this case, they are not really idle, although their chances of future economic success are lower than those of young women who are working or in school. Thus, a final indicator of future well-being among young women is *early childbearing*. Young women who become mothers while still in their teens are less likely to graduate from high school on time and less likely to go on to college than young women who delay childbearing. They are also less likely to be in the labor force. While much of the association between early childbearing and educational attainment may be due to differences in family background rather than to teen motherhood itself, there is little doubt that early childbearing reduces a young woman's chances of becoming an economically independent adult.[8] Over two thirds of teen mothers are unmarried when their child is born,[9] and the other third have a high risk of divorce. Since the fathers of these children are rarely able or willing to provide financial support to help cover the costs of childrearing, a majority of teen mothers are forced to depend on welfare. Many stay on welfare until their children are grown.[10] Welfare mothers live at or below the poverty line and are treated with very little respect. Nor do they have much control over their lives, given the numerous eligibility requirements attached to welfare receipt and the continuing threat of benefit cuts.

While teenage childbearing is much less common today than it was in 1960 or 1970, the costs to young women of early motherhood—like the costs of dropping out of high school—have gone up.[11] Certainly, the economic consequences for society are greater today than they were thirty years ago, when most teenage mothers (over two thirds) were married and were supported by their husbands.[12]

## HOW PARENTS PROMOTE
## CHILDREN'S SUCCESS

In order to grow up to be successful adults, children need intellectual stimulation, and they need to know that working hard and getting a good education will pay off in the future. They also need a close relationship with a parent who is committed to their well-being and who has the ability and authority to supervise their activities and make sure they do not "get off on the wrong track" inadvertently. Finally young people need adults outside the family who care about them, who support their parents, and who are in a position to help them find jobs and get established in the adult world.[13]

Parents bear primary responsibility for making sure that children's needs are met. They are the ones who determine how much time and money is devoted to children's education and intellectual development. They are the ones who provide guidance and supervision. And they are the ones who provide the connections to adults and institutions outside the family that are critical both in maintaining social control and in providing children with information about the labor market. When parents live apart, these processes and activities are undermined and in some instances destroyed. This occurs primarily through a loss of economic, parental, and community resources.

## Loss of Economic Resources

Nowhere is the lack of resources among children in one-parent families more evident than in the official poverty statistics reported by the U.S. Bureau of the Census. In 1992 approximately 45 percent of families with children headed by single mothers were living below the poverty line, as compared with 8.4 percent of families with two parents.[14] Nor is this disparity limited to a particular point in time. Single-mother families have had higher poverty rates than other families for as far back as we have data on poverty and family income.

Of course, the high poverty rate of single-mother families cannot be blamed entirely on family structure. Some single mothers who are living below the poverty line were poor prior to the breakup of their family. Mary Jo Bane has estimated that about 65 percent of all new cases of poverty among black women who go from a married-couple family to a female-headed family are instances of *reshuffled poverty.* Among white women the figure is much lower— only 25 percent were poor prior to the breakup of their marriage.[15] And these figures do not include never-married mothers, who are even more likely to come from disadvantaged backgrounds than divorced, separated, or widowed mothers. The fact that many women are poor when they become single mothers, however, does not mean that they do not fall even further below the poverty line as a consequence of separation or divorce. Nor does it mean that their chances of escaping poverty are not lower after a separation. In any given year, married-couple families are much more likely to move out of poverty than single-mother families.[16]

Even children from advantaged backgrounds experience a loss of economic resources when their parents live apart. The average decline in income of a mother and child who are living in a nonpoor family prior to separation is 50 percent. And these children experience ongoing economic instability, as single mothers go in and out of the labor force and as they form and dissolve new intimate relationships.

Does family disruption always lead to a loss of economic resources? While no law says that single parents must have lower income than married parents, many factors make this outcome very likely. When parents live apart, they are supporting two households rather than one, which means that they forgo economies of scale—gains from sharing expenses. The biggest savings come from sharing housing costs. But even food is cheaper per person when more people are splitting the bill. Of course if all divorces (or terminated partnerships) resulted in remarriages (or new partnerships), there would be no loss of economies of scale. But this is not what usually happens. Although some single mothers remarry, a substantial proportion do not, and most of those who remain single head their own household.[17]

To get an idea of the economic costs of *not* pooling resources, consider what it takes to support a family of four (two parents and two children) under different living arrangements.[18] When the parents and children live together, the family needs $14,228 to live above the poverty line, according to the official government definition of poverty. If the parents live in separate households and both children live with the mother, the family needs $18,603 to maintain the same standard of living for all members: $11,304 for the mother and children, and $7,299 for the father. It does not matter which parent lives with the children; the total cost of maintaining two households above the poverty line is the same. For a family of four, the economies of scale are worth over $4,000.

Loss of economies of scale, however, is not the only reason children's standard of living declines after a divorce or separation. Equally important is the fact that total family income is not distributed equally when parents live apart. A mother and children usually receive less than half the total family income, even though their household has more people, whereas the father usually receives more than half of the total income, even though his household has fewer people. The consequence of this unequal division of resources can be seen by comparing the standard of living of fathers and mothers after divorce. The economic status of divorced mothers usually goes down after divorce, whereas the status of divorced fathers goes up.[19]

A major reason family income is unevenly distributed across households is that many nonresident fathers do not pay adequate child support. About 40 percent of children who are theoretically eligible for child support do not have a child support award at all, and a quarter of those with an award receive nothing. Less than a third of children receive the full amount they are owed.

The fact that such a small percentage of children receive adequate child support is due in part to the weakness of our current child support system and in part to the social norms that lie beneath this system. According to Irwin Garfinkel, the system is unfair and condones parental irresponsibility.[20] It is unfair because it treats fathers in identical circumstances differently. Some fathers have financial obligations that amount to a huge percentage of their income, while others have relatively small obligations. The system condones parental irresponsibility because it does a poor job of collecting child support from uncooperative fathers. The fact that child support awards are perceived as unfair and local enforcement is weak makes it easier for nonresident fathers to avoid their responsibilities. Indeed, given the sad state of our current system, it is remarkable that a third of nonresident fathers pay in full on a regular basis! These fathers are a testament to the strong commitment some nonresident parents have to their children.

In addition to a lack of social enforcement, another reason nonresident fathers are reluctant to support their children is that the economic costs and the psychological benefits of children change after divorce. The economist Gary Becker suggests that fathers who live in separate households become less altruistic toward (or less closely identified with) their children over time, which makes them less willing to share their income with them.[21] Absence seems to make the heart grow weaker, according to this theory. Sometimes nonresident fathers feel less altruistic toward their children because they see them less often and are less aware of their needs. Some fathers may develop new emotional attachments which supersede their previous commitments to their children.

Other economists argue that fathers do not pay child support because they are unable to monitor and control how the money is spent. Weiss and Willis show that in order to contribute a dollar to the child, a nonresident parent must pay more than a dollar, since some of the money goes toward the support of the custodial parent and other members of her household rather than the child. Faced with these domestic realities, many fathers respond by paying less child support.[22]

Both of these explanations—loss of commitment and loss of trust—are consistent with the notion that father absence leads to a loss of social capital for the child.[23] These losses are experienced not just by children who lived with their fathers for some time before the breakup but also by children who have never lived with their fathers. From our perspective, both groups of children "lose" something when their parents decide to live separately: they lose what might have been. For this reason, throughout this discussion and in the sections that follow, unless we indicate otherwise, these two groups of children will be treated the same way.

### Loss of Parental Resources

Children have less access to parental resources when their fathers live in separate households. Indeed, the loss of parental resources is partly responsible for the loss of economic resources, if we are correct about how social capital works. Fathers who live in separate households see their children less often,[24] and this may undermine commitment and trust. Interacting with the former spouse and building a new relationship with the child can be a difficult and painful experience, and many fathers respond by disengaging from their children.[25] Children also have strong feelings about the separation, which may further damage the already weakened father-child relationship. Most children are angry when their parents separate; many feel betrayed and abandoned by their fathers, even in families where the parents' decision was mutual or where the father did not want the separation.[26] Since the mother usually retains custody of the children, the father is often perceived as leaving the family, and the child's anger is often directed at him. If the parents are angry at each other, as is frequently the case, they may communicate this anger to the child, who may feel torn in two directions. Even in families where the separation is amicable, nearly all children feel uncertain about how family members should relate to one another in the future. No matter what happens, children's trust has been seriously shaken.

We should point out that children who never lived with their fathers or never knew their fathers do not feel the same kind of anger as children who experience their parents' separation directly. This is one case where the experience of children who never knew their fathers is quite different from that of children who knew and lived with their fathers.

Some fathers argue that they would like to see their children more often but are prevented from doing so by mothers. Just as social norms governing the economic obligations of nonresident fathers are weak, norms governing fathers' rights are also weak. Most states do not actively enforce a father's right to spend time with his child, nor do they prevent mothers from moving out of state. Even social service professionals may discourage fathers from maintaining contact with the child if they believe that contact will lead to conflict between the parents.[27]

In addition to altering the relationship between fathers and children, family disruption affects the mother–child relationship. Most single mothers are forced to fill two roles simultaneously, without adequate support. Not surprisingly, some experience high levels of stress and become anxious and depressed.[28] This can lead to inconsistent parenting, which makes it difficult to provide the kind of discipline coupled with affection that children need. Rather than developing an authoritative parenting style (firm discipline combined with warmth), which child development experts tell us is the best way to raise children, some mothers become overly permissive (too little discipline), while others become overly authoritarian (too little warmth). Neither of these last two parenting styles is good for children.[29]

While some of the problems that arise from stress may improve over time, as mothers learn to cope with their new responsibilities, other problems are rooted in the structure of the one-parent family itself.[30] Despite its many weaknesses, the nuclear family is a pretty good system for making sure that parents invest in their children and that children obey their parents. When two biological parents share the same household, they can monitor the children and maintain parental control. But just as important, the parents also can monitor one another and make sure the other parent is behaving in appropriate ways. Parents do not always feel like taking time out of their busy schedules to read to their children or take part in afterschool activities. Having another parent around who cares about the child increases the likelihood that each parent will "do the right thing" even when otherwise inclined. In short, the two-parent family structure creates a system of checks and balances that both promotes parental responsibility and protects the child from parental neglect and, sometimes, abuse.[31] This is an important function of social capital within the family.

Of course not all nuclear families work this way. Sometimes parents are unable to cooperate in raising their children, and sometimes they just don't care whether or not they do a good job. In such households, parenting is likely to be poor and authority is likely to be weak, regardless of whether the parents live together or apart. But dismantling a faulty system does not ensure that a better one will take its place. Parental authority is likely to remain weak in a one-parent family, since monitoring is much more difficult for one parent than for two. And parental affection and warmth is also likely to be below average, since the mother must fill two roles instead of one and is likely to be under considerable stress.

In some families the oldest child, or the oldest daughter, may become a confidant of the mother and act as a surrogate parent for her younger siblings.[32] While such an arrangement may provide comfort to the mother and may reinforce parental authority, it is unlikely to be as effective as having two parents in the household. Moreover, it does not provide authority or protection for the eldest child.

In families where the mother remarries or cohabits with an adult male, the quality of parenting is still likely to be lower than in families with two biological parents. From the child's point of view, having a new adult move into the household creates another disruption. Having adjusted to the father's moving out, the child must now experience a second reorganization of household personnel.[33] Stepfathers are less likely to be committed to the child's welfare than biological fathers, and they are less likely to serve as a check on the mother's behavior. Rather than assisting with the responsibilities of parenting, stepfathers sometimes compete with the child for the mother's time, adding to the mother's and the child's level of stress.

Even when a stepfather tries to play an active role in parenting the child, his efforts may be rejected or undermined by the mother because she is reluctant to share authority or because she does not trust his judgment. Children may reject their stepfathers because they resent having to share their mothers, or because they feel loyalty toward their fathers, or because they secretly hope their biological parents will get back together. The fact that stepparents are almost always portrayed as evil in children's fairy tales is indicative of the widespread mistrust associated with the stepparent role. In cohabiting unions, issues of authority and trust are even more problematic.

What about grandmothers? Can they substitute for absent fathers? Can they make life easier for single mothers? At first glance, having a grandmother in the household seems like a good idea, since grandmothers are in a position to reinforce the mother's authority and are likely to feel committed to their grandchildren. Similarly, children are more likely to trust a grandmother than a new stepfather because they know the grandmother better and are less likely to feel that she is competing with them for the mother's attention. While in the past some researchers have found that children raised by single mothers and grandmothers did nearly as well as children raised by two parents,[34] recent studies suggest that this view may be overly optimistic. In their study of multigenerational African American families, Lindsay Chase-Lansdale and her colleagues found that the quality of parenting was lower in multigenerational families than in single-mother families. They concluded that "shared parenting" often led to conflict between the mother and grandmother and to a diffusion of parental responsibility which, in turn, undermined the quality of parenting from both the mother and grandmother.[35]

In sum, while it is certainly not impossible for two adults other than a mother and father to raise a child successfully, the chances of this happening are not as great as they are in a two-parent family. As we will show in the following chapters, the average child raised in a stepfamily or by a mother and grandmother is doing about the same as the average child raised by a single mother.

### What about Parental Conflict?

Thus far we have been talking about how parents' decision to live apart reduces children's access to parental resources. Yet some people believe that children in divorced families had fewer parental resources than other children even before their parents separated. According to this view, whatever caused the father to leave the household in the first place may have been affecting the father-child relationship even before he left.

Parental conflict is often cited as a cause of both family disruption and the loss of parental resources. We know that children raised in high-conflict families have more problems than children raised in low-conflict families, and we also know that parental conflict often leads to divorce.[36] However, before we can say that parental conflict is the principal explanation for why children from divorced families are less successful than children from intact families, several factors must be taken into account.

First, we must know something about the source and degree of conflict. If the father has severe personality problems and is violent or abusive toward the child or mother, the father-child relationship will be damaged regardless of whether the parents live together or apart. Indeed, the child may be better off if the parents separate. On the other hand, if both parents are reasonable people and care about the child, and if conflict arises because one (or both) of the parents is bored with the marriage or falls in love with someone else, the answer to the question "What is best for the child?" is less clear. From the child's point of view, these two types of conflict (abuse versus weak commitment) are very different matters. In the latter case, the child would probably be better off if the parents resolved their differences and the family remained together, even if the long-term relationship between the parents was less than perfect.

Second, we need to ask whether the parents' separation puts an end to conflict or whether it increases conflict. Sometimes parents continue their disputes after the father moves out, and sometimes new conflicts develop between mothers and other adults in the household, such as stepfathers, unmarried partners, or grandmothers.[37] We know from previous studies that postdivorce conflict between the biological parents or between mothers and stepfathers has negative consequences for children.

Third, the effects of conflict must be evaluated along with other factors that are triggered by family disruption. While family disruption may end hostilities between the parents, making children better off despite the loss of parental resources, it may reduce their economic and community resources, making them worse off. Even in high-conflict situations, all these factors must be weighed in deciding whether divorce does more harm than good.

### Loss of Community Resources

A final way that father absence affects children is by lowering their access to community resources. This occurs in two ways. The first is primarily an income effect. Families with more income can afford to live in communities with better facilities, and since single parenthood reduces income, it also restricts single-parent families to communities where resources are low.[38]

Divorce and separation also reduce children's connections to their community. Just as strong parent-child relationships provide children with social capital, so do strong community connections.

When parents and children live in a community for a long time, they develop close ties that provide emotional support as well as information about the broader community. When a family moves from town to town or from neighborhood to neighborhood, these ties are undermined and often destroyed.

Children of divorced and separated parents move more often than children in intact families.[39] In part the changes in residence are due to changes in family size. When the father moves out of the house, the family needs less space, and the mother may choose to move to a less expensive dwelling. When the mother remarries or when a boyfriend or grandmother moves in, space needs increase, and the family may move again. Changes in mothers' employment may also necessitate a move. Regardless of the cause, frequent moving undermines social capital because long-term relationships of commitment and trust cannot develop.

Divorce and single parenthood may undermine community connections even when the family does not move. Parents may disengage from their old friends after a divorce or separation, either because past memories are painful or because new associations are more attractive.[40] And this may leave children feeling cut off from friends and neighbors. While new relationships, from the parent's point of view, may be a good way of coping with the pain of separation and the strain of building a new life, from the child's point of view they are unlikely to be positive experiences. Most children going through a divorce are trying to keep their old world intact.

Other single mothers may be so stressed, or depressed, after a divorce that they simply do not have the time or energy to invest in personal relationships, and so let old friends drift away and fail to develop new ones. In either case, the loss of family ties reduces children's social capital.

## HOW THE LOSS OF RESOURCES AFFECTS CHILD WELL-BEING

In the previous discussion we showed how family disruption leads to a loss of economic, parental, and community resources. Now we describe how the loss of these three types of resources lowers children's school performance, decreases their labor force attachment, and contributes to early childbearing. The examples provided below are not intended to cover all areas of a child's life that are affected by family disruption. Rather they simply illustrate the types of mechanisms through which the loss of resources leads to lower child well-being.

*Schooling Achievement*

Perhaps the most obvious way in which income loss affects children's educational achievement is by lowering the quality of the schools they attend. Parents with high incomes can afford to live in neighborhoods with good public schools, or they can send their children to private schools, whichever they prefer. In contrast, parents with limited incomes have fewer options, and their children generally attend lower quality schools.

Income also affects whether or not parents can afford to pay for lessons after school and whether they can take their children on trips or send them to camp during the summer. These extracurricular activities not only improve children's skills, they also provide general intellectual stimulation, which affects subsequent learning. Indeed, a major problem faced by teachers who work with economically disadvantaged children is the loss of learning (in a relative as well as an absolute sense) that occurs over the summer holidays for children from disadvantaged backgrounds.[41]

Apart from income, the loss of parental time affects school achievement. Children whose parents read to them and take an interest in their schoolwork do better in school than children whose parents are distracted and less involved. Nonresident parents are not available to help with homework. Resident parents are often overwhelmed by their multiple responsibilities and cannot do as much as they would like.

The lack of parental involvement in schooling is especially important for children from economically disadvantaged backgrounds. Ethnographic studies of minority families and poor immigrant families contain numerous examples of how parents promote their children's school achievement in the face of great odds by stressing the importance of schoolwork and by creating a supportive work environment in the home. In his study of poor black families, Reginald Clark provides examples of both single parents and married parents who are heavily involved in their children's schoolwork and whose children are doing unusually well in school.[42] He argues that parental support is much more important than the number of parents in the household in determining school success. While Clark is undoubtedly correct about the importance of parental support, on average children from single-parent families are less likely to have a supportive environment.

Access to community resources can affect children's educational experiences, independent of parents' income and time. Consider two children living in the same neighborhood. One family has lived in the neighborhood for ten years; the other has lived there for less than a year. The parents of the first child are likely to be more knowledgeable about the educational resources in the community and to be in a better position to take advantage of these resources than the parents of the second child. The more established parents know the names of the good teachers, and they know the ones to avoid. They are also familiar with afterschool activities and know how to gain access to the ones in short supply. In other words, the first family has much more social capital than the second, and we would expect the children in the first family to receive a better education than the children in the second, even though they live in the same neighborhood and attend the same school.

Finally, the loss of economic and social resources affects children's willingness to invest in themselves, by lowering expectations and reducing motivation. Young adults who do not expect to go to college, even though they clearly have the ability, are less motivated to work hard in high school than youngsters who expect to go on to college. In large part, lower expectations reflect the lack of income that is common among children in single-parent families. But other factors play a role as well. Children who live apart from their father are less certain of their parents' willingness to financially support their efforts to go to college, and this affects their expectations and motivation. Children whose fathers have not been paying child support on a regular basis in the past are unlikely to expect much help from their fathers in the future. (Recall that over half of nonresident parents pay no child support.) Moreover, children living in stepfamilies may feel uncertain about their stepfathers' support, because their relationship is weak or strained or because the stepfather is supporting children in another household.

We are not suggesting that nonresident fathers or stepfathers never help pay for their children's college education or that fathers in two-parent families always pay for college. Clearly, neither of these statements is true. Our point is simply that, holding constant fathers' ability to pay, children are much more likely to receive help from biological fathers living in the household than from fathers who are not when it comes time to pay college tuition.

## Labor Force Attachment

Clearly the educational deficits described above are a major reason children with only one parent in the home have more trouble finding and keeping a steady job than children from two-parent families. But education is not the only factor that determines whether or not a young man or woman is able to get off on the right vocational track.

Many jobs are found through networks and local connections. And here the lack of parental resources can be just as damaging as the lack of income. Whereas the typical adolescent in a two-parent family has two employed parents to help counsel her on finding a job, the typical child in a single-parent family often has only one working parent, and some children have no working parent. Clearly children whose fathers do not reside in the household are at a great disadvantage relative to peers with fathers at home when it comes to finding a job, not only because they are less likely to know about job openings but also because they may not know how to apply for a job and how to conduct themselves during interviews.

In addition to the lack of parental resources, the lack of community resources also weakens children's connection to the labor force. Children who live in very poor communities where many adults are jobless and on welfare have less information about how to find a job than children who live in prosperous communities. And children whose families move around a lot are less likely to ask their neighbors for help in finding a job.

In his study of three low-income communities in the New York City area, Mercer Sullivan describes how job networks can affect the transition from school to work.[43] In one community where employment rates among adult males are high and community solidarity is strong, young men, including those without a high school diploma, are able to find work. In another community where male employment rates are low and where there is a lack of solidarity, young men, even those who have a high school diploma, have much more difficulty finding work. While Sullivan's study was based on three low-income communities, his underlying message applies to middle-class communities as well. Social connections are an important resource when it comes to finding a steady job.

## Early Childbearing

Living with a single parent affects early family formation via two routes. First, it lowers family income, which reduces a young woman's assessment of the costs of early childbearing. A teenager who does not expect to go to college or to have an interesting job is much less motivated to avoid or terminate a pregnancy than a young woman who has many opportunities and who expects to pursue a career.

A second way in which the loss of resources encourages early childbearing is by reducing social control and increasing opportunities for engaging in irresponsible sexual activity. Here, the word "irresponsible" refers to unprotected sexual intercourse and the failure to financially support a child once it is born. While some young women do act rationally—weighing the costs and benefits of their opportunities as they perceive them—when deciding whether or not to use contraceptives, young people do not always act in their long-term self-interest, as anyone who has raised a child or worked closely with a teenager knows. More often than not, teenage sexual behavior is governed by impulse and fantasy. Viewed in this way, early childbearing is very much a consequence of parents' failure to monitor their children and to impose sanctions on irresponsible behavior.[44] If parents are not watchful, children are likely to make foolish mistakes, regardless of the long-term costs.

It is easy to understand how parents who are experiencing high levels of stress or who are trying to raise their children alone might have more difficulty monitoring their children than parents who are not experiencing stress and who are able to cooperate with one another and share the burden of vigilance. It is also easy to see why single mothers might find it harder than married mothers to constrain their children's behavior, even if they know their children are acting irresponsibly. With less backup from nonresident fathers and from other adults in the community, they have more difficulty disciplining their children than married parents.

In addition, single parents may inadvertently encourage teenage sexual activity by acting as role models. Single mothers who are dating or cohabiting, for example, send a message to their teenage daughters that sex outside marriage is acceptable and perhaps even preferable. In his longitudinal study of mother-daughter pairs, Arland Thornton found that daughters of divorced mothers held more liberal views about sex outside marriage than daughters of married mothers. This was even more pronounced among daughters of remarried mothers, which suggests that it is mothers' postdivorce dating behavior that shapes daughters' attitudes rather than the marital disruption itself.[45] Even more important, nonresident fathers may also act as role models for their sons and make it easier for young men to shirk their parental responsibilities. A father who does not support his own children sends a message to his son (and daughter) that children are women's responsibility, not men's. In doing so, he makes it harder for the resident parent, or anyone else, to control his son's behavior and to insist that the son take responsibility for his decisions.

Elijah Anderson presents a vivid description of such a community in his study of the "sexual games" young men and women play in a poor innercity neighborhood.[46] In Anderson's community, the young women dream of marriage and middle-class lifestyles, while the young men exploit the girls' fantasies in order to gain sexual favors and status with their peers. Not surprisingly, the game leads to a high rate of teenage motherhood and a high rate of abandonment by fathers. What is most striking about Anderson's account is not the romantic notions of the young women nor the willingness of the young men to exploit these fantasies to satisfy their own desires. Such fantasies and games are familiar to most Americans. What is striking is that the game he describes is played with no adult referees in sight. In Anderson's community, the parents have abdicated their responsibility for protecting their daughters and for insisting that their sons accept responsibility for the children they conceive.

If we were asked to design a system for making sure that children's basic needs were met, we would probably come up with something quite similar to the two-parent family ideal. Such a design, in theory, would not only ensure that children had access to the time and money of two adults, it also would provide a system of checks and balances that promoted quality parenting. The fact that both adults have a biological connection to the child would increase the likelihood that the parents would identify with the child and be willing to sacrifice for that child, and it would reduce the likelihood that either parent would abuse the child. Last but not least, the fact that two parents had connections to the community would increase the child's access to information about opportunities outside the household and would, at the same time, strengthen social control. While we recognize that two-parent families frequently do not live up to this ideal in all respects, nevertheless we would expect children who grow up in two-parent families to be doing better, on average, than children who grow up with only one parent. In the chapters that follow we will test these expectations against the evidence.

# CHAPTER THREE

# WHICH OUTCOMES ARE MOST AFFECTED

Finishing school, finding a job, and starting a family are events that mark the transition from adolescence to adulthood. For many children, this transition is not an easy one. Some stop school prematurely because they feel hopeless about the future or because other activities seem more important at the time. Some young girls become mothers while they are still children, and in doing so put themselves at risk for long-term poverty and dependence. Finally, many young people have trouble finding steady employment. Some are idle for several years after leaving school. Others work intermittently. Getting off on the wrong track during the transition from adolescence to adulthood is not fatal, but getting started on the right track makes life a lot easier later on.

In this chapter we present evidence to show that children who grow up with both parents are more successful in making the transition from adolescence to adulthood than children who grow up with only one parent. We examine a broad range of outcomes, and we assess the magnitude of the effects as well as the breadth. We also examine whether boys and girls—and children from different racial and social class backgrounds—respond differently to living with a single parent.

We begin by contrasting children who live with both biological parents with all other children, holding constant other differences in family characteristics such as race, parents' education, family size, residential location, and sometimes ability. Since we cannot adjust for every possible difference between families that break up and those that stay together, we cannot say with certainty that the children from disrupted families would have done the same as children from two-parent families (and vice versa) had their situations been reversed. However, given the size and consistency of the differences in child outcomes, we believe that parents and policymakers cannot afford to ignore the possibility that a substantial portion of these differences are due to family disruption and father absence.

## EDUCATIONAL ACHIEVEMENT

It is useful to think of educational achievement as a series of transitions, beginning with high school graduation and continuing through college entry and college graduation. Different transitions have different implications for long-term economic security. Dropping out of high school, for example, is an event with serious and long-term negative consequences. If we want to know whether divorce produces long-term poverty and welfare dependence, this is the educational transition to focus on. Graduating from college, on the other hand, is an event with more positive implications. If we want to know whether divorce is related to economic prosperity, college graduation is the indicator to look at.

### Dropping Out of High School

The overwhelming majority of young people in the United States graduate from high school. About 73 percent receive a high school diploma, and another 12 percent receive a General Equivalency Diploma (GED). Altogether, only 15 percent of young adults fail to graduate from high school by the time they reach adulthood.[1]

While dropping out of school is a relatively uncommon event, the risk of dropping out is much higher for children who grow up with only one parent as compared with children who live with both biological parents. Figure 1 shows the high school dropout rates of young adults from two-parent families and one-parent families.[2]

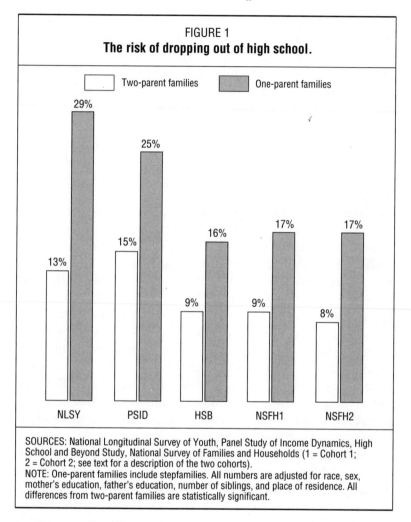

FIGURE 1
**The risk of dropping out of high school.**

SOURCES: National Longitudinal Survey of Youth, Panel Study of Income Dynamics, High School and Beyond Study, National Survey of Families and Households (1 = Cohort 1; 2 = Cohort 2; see text for a description of the two cohorts).
NOTE: One-parent families include stepfamilies. All numbers are adjusted for race, sex, mother's education, father's education, number of siblings, and place of residence. All differences from two-parent families are statistically significant.

Regardless of which survey we look at, children from one-parent families are about twice as likely to drop out of school as children from two-parent families. In the National Longitudinal Survey of Young Men and Women (NLSY), the dropout rate is 29 percent for children from one-parent families, as compared with 13 percent for children from two-parent families. In the Panel Study of Income

Dynamics (PSID), the rates are 25 percent and 15 percent. The rates are lower in the High School and Beyond Study (HSB)—16 percent and 9 percent respectively—because the HSB is a school-based survey, and young people who stop school prior to the tenth grade are not included in the sample. We would expect students who make it to the sophomore year to have a lower dropout rate than all children.

The rates are also lower in the two National Survey of Families and Households samples, but for a different reason. Graduation is measured as of the time of the survey (1987) rather than at age twenty. Thus, the respondents had more time to graduate or obtain an equivalency diploma than the respondents in the other surveys.[3]

The difference between children in two-parent and one-parent families is even larger when we exclude GEDs and use only a high school diploma as our indicator of school success. In the NLSY the difference is 22 rather than 16 percentage points; in the HSB study it is 10 rather than 7; and in the NSFH Cohort 1, it is 15 points rather than 8. This greater difference means that children from disrupted families make up some of the difference in school achievement by obtaining a GED. This is reassuring insofar as it indicates that children who stop school prematurely have a second chance to get their diplomas. On the other hand, if a GED turns out to be a second-rate diploma, as some economists have suggested, the numbers we report in Figure 1 are underestimates of the negative consequences of family disruption.[4]

Clearly, living with only one biological parent increases a child's chances of dropping out of high school. But how are we to evaluate the magnitude of the difference? Is a doubling of the risk of a relatively rare event a large or small effect? Unfortunately, this question does not have a simple answer. One way to assess the magnitude of the family structure effect is to compare the disadvantage associated with living in a one-parent family with the disadvantage associated with having a mother who has not finished high school. A mother's education is generally regarded as the single best predictor of a child's school achievement, and thus it provides a good benchmark against which to evaluate the importance of other variables.

If we compare the effect of family structure on high school graduation with the effect of the mother's education, we find that the two are about the same. Having a mother with less than a high school degree, as compared with having a mother with a high school degree, doubles the risk of dropping out of school.[5] Since most people would agree that the mother's education is an important factor in children's educational achievement, they probably would also agree that family structure is an important factor.

Another way of assessing the importance of family structure is to ask how much lower the dropout rate in the overall population would be if *all* children lived with both parents. If we use the numbers from the NLSY survey, the answer to this question is 6 percentage points. If there were no one-parent families and if all children currently in one-parent families did as well as children in two-parent families, the dropout rate for the country as a whole would fall from 19 to 13 percent. Viewed in this way, family disruption accounts for about a third of the overall high school dropout rate.

These comparisons illustrate the difficulty in trying to assess the importance of family disruption, and they explain why analysts often disagree about the size of the effect. If we want to know whether living with only one parent increases the risk of dropping out of school, the answer is clearly yes. On the other hand, if we want to know whether it is the primary source of school failure, the answer is clearly no.

*Early Disengagement from School*
Dropping out of high school often signifies the end of a process of disengagement that begins long before the student actually stops going to school. Thus, one might ask whether children in two-parent families and one-parent families are different prior to leaving high school. If differences in school performance arise several years prior to the projected graduation date, this would tell us something about the mechanisms underlying the association between family structure and school success.

For example, if children from disrupted families drop out of

TABLE 1
**Differences in high school performance of children raised
in two-parent and one-parent families.**

| Family type | Test score | School attitude | College expectations | Grade-point average | School attendance |
|---|---|---|---|---|---|
| Two-parent families | 2.62 | 80.4% | 37.5% | 4.13 | 9.83 |
| One-parent families | **2.51** | 80.1 | **32.2** | **3.92** | **9.25** |

*Source:* High School and Beyond Study.
*Note:* See text for explanation of categories. One-parent families include
stepfamilies. All numbers are adjusted for race, sex, mother's education,
father's education, number of siblings, and place of residence. Statistically
significant differences from two-parent families are in bold type.

school prematurely because they are less talented than children from
two-parent families, we would expect to find differences in the test
scores of these children prior to dropping out. If, on the other hand,
children in one-parent families are just as talented as their peers
but are forced to stop school prematurely in order to help support
their families or provide childcare for younger siblings, we would
expect to find similar test scores prior to dropping out.

Table 1 contains data on five different indicators of school performance: standardized test scores, attitudes toward schoolwork,
college expectations, grade-point average, and school attendance.
*Test score* measures whether a student ranks in the first (lowest),
second, third, or fourth (top) quartile of his or her class, based on
nationally standardized tests in reading, vocabulary, and mathemat-
ics. *School attitude* measures whether a student likes school and will
be disappointed if he or she does not graduate from college. *College
expectations* distinguishes between students who expect to go to
college and students who do not. *Grade-point average* is based on a
seven-point scale. A score of seven indicates an A average, six indicates A/B, five indicates B, four indicates B/C, three indicates C,

and so on. *School attendance* measures whether a student was late or absent from school during the past two months. A score of 12 indicates a perfect record; a score of 0 indicates that a student was absent or late all of the time. As before, all of the estimates reported in the table have been adjusted to take race, parents' education, family size, and region of the country into account.

Children from one-parent families do less well than their peers on four out of five indicators. Their test scores are lower, their expectations about college are lower, their grades are lower, and their attendance record is poorer. The only indicator that does not show a significant disadvantage for students in one-parent families is the school attitude measure. Children from one-parent families are just as likely to report that they like school and want to go to college as children from two-parent families.

Notice that children's expectations about going to college do not match their school attitudes very well. Nearly all children—80 percent in both types of families—say they like school and want to go to college, but less than 40 percent say they *expect* to go to college. Expectations are lower among children from disrupted families as compared with children from two-parent families (37 versus 32 percent), which is what we would expect, given their more limited economic resources. Indeed, we were surprised to find that as many as a third of children from one-parent families expected to go to college. As we will see, these students were not very far off the mark—family disruption reduced their chances of going to college by about 5 percentage points.

Children from disrupted families are clearly different from their peers prior to high school graduation in more ways than simply talent or ability. Students in one-parent families have lower grades and poorer attendance records than children in two-parent families, even after test scores for aptitude are taken into account.[6] The fact that differences in grades and attendance persist after adjusting for test scores is troubling because it suggests that children from one-parent families are not as motivated to work hard in school as children from two-parent families. Ability is important, but hard work and discipline are also essential for success. Thus, single parenthood reduces children's chances in at least two ways: by lowering their aptitude for school and by lowering their motivation as well. Moreover, a poor attendance record not only tells us that a child is not doing well in school but also sends a signal that a child may be involved in delinquent or other potentially harmful activities outside school. Children with poor attendance records are usually children with other behavioral problems.

At this point we cannot say why some children from disrupted families are doing poorly in school. Their relatively poor aptitude and performance could be due to low income or poor parenting or to something about the quality of the school itself. Moreover, the reasons may not be the same for all children, since no two families are exactly alike. Some children in disrupted families may be doing poorly in school because they are trying to hold down an outside job to help support their families. Others may be doing poorly because they are not getting enough support and supervision from their mothers, and still others may feel alienated from school because of conflict at home or because they have recently moved to a new school and left their old friends. We will investigate some of these possibilities in the next few chapters.

### College Attendance and College Graduation

How does family structure affect higher education? On the one hand, we might expect it to have a greater effect on college attainment than on high school graduation, since going to college poses a more serious economic barrier for a family than finishing high school. On the other hand, we might expect the effect to be weaker, since students with the least ability and the most serious behavioral problems do not finish high school and are not eligible to go to college. They are weeded out of the system, so to speak, prior to college.

Figure 2 reports college enrollment and graduation figures for children from two-parent and one-parent families. The number at the top of each bar represents the percentage of high school graduates that enrolled in college, and the number near the center of the bar represents the percentage of high school graduates that finished

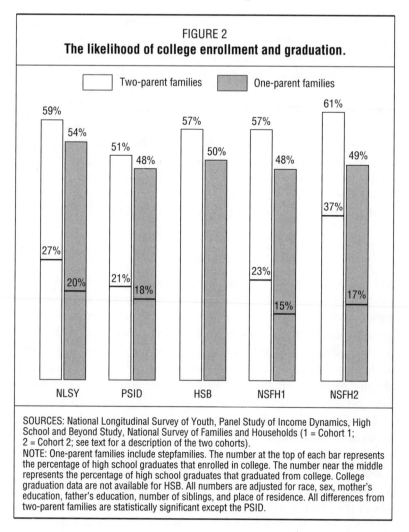

## FIGURE 2
**The likelihood of college enrollment and graduation.**

☐ Two-parent families   ▨ One-parent families

|  | NLSY | PSID | HSB | NSFH1 | NSFH2 |
|--|------|------|-----|-------|-------|

SOURCES: National Longitudinal Survey of Youth, Panel Study of Income Dynamics, High School and Beyond Study, National Survey of Families and Households (1 = Cohort 1; 2 = Cohort 2; see text for a description of the two cohorts).
NOTE: One-parent families include stepfamilies. The number at the top of each bar represents the percentage of high school graduates that enrolled in college. The number near the middle represents the percentage of high school graduates that graduated from college. College graduation data are not available for HSB. All numbers are adjusted for race, sex, mother's education, father's education, number of siblings, and place of residence. All differences from two-parent families are statistically significant except the PSID.

college. As before, the results have been adjusted for differences in family background characteristics.[7] The numbers show that the disadvantage associated with family disruption persists beyond the high school years. The negative effect of family structure, however, is somewhat smaller on college enrollment and graduation than it is on high school graduation. Family disruption reduces a child's chances of enrolling in college by about 5 percentage points, according to the NLSY, and it reduces his chances of graduating later on by about 7 percentage points. The percentages are somewhat higher in the HSB and NSFH surveys and somewhat lower in the PSID, where they are not statistically significant. But overall, the basic message is the same: family disruption continues to reduce children's school achievement after high school. As we shall see at the end of the chapter, the effects of family disruption on college graduation are larger for children from advantaged families as compared with children from the average family, and there is some evidence that they are larger for young women than young men.

### IDLENESS

For young adults who do not go to college, work experience and on-the-job training are other ways of building skills and increasing productivity. Thus, if we are concerned about a person's future economic security, we must ask whether someone who does not attend college is able to find and hold a steady job after high school. Individuals who are not going to school or building their skills during early adulthood are likely to have employment problems later on.

Most young men are either working or in school in their late teens and early twenties. Only about 15 percent of the young men in the NLSY survey, and only 12 percent of those in the HSB study, were idle in the first few years after high school. The PSID sample yielded a much higher rate of idleness than the other two surveys—about 25 percent of the young men in that sample were neither working nor in school. Our measures of idleness are somewhat different in each of the surveys, which is one reason the levels fluctuate so much (see Appendix A). Another reason is the ambiguity of the word "idleness." A person who is on vacation or planning to start work next week, for example, may not know how to respond to the question, "Are you currently employed?"

What is important is that the effects of family disruption on idleness are consistent across the different surveys. Young men from one-parent families are about 1.5 times as likely to be idle as young men from two-parent families, regardless of which survey we look at. To make sure that the association between family structure and idleness was not simply due to the fact that young men from one-parent families were more likely to have dropped out of high school, we restricted our sample to those who had completed high school. The difference in the risk of being idle between children in two-parent and one-parent families was virtually the same, as shown in Figure 3, even after high school dropouts were excluded from the sample. This means that growing up in a disrupted family affects young men's future success in at least two different ways: by reducing the chances of finishing high school and by reducing labor force attachment.

We also looked at whether test scores might account for some of the association between family structure and idleness among boys. As in the case of high school graduation, we found that variation in test scores accounted for about 20 percent of the higher incidence of idleness among children in one-parent families. In other words, factors besides innate ability must be found to account for four fifths of the difference.

The fact that the relationship between family structure and high school graduation and work does not disappear among boys once we adjust for test scores is important and relates back to our theory of why growing up in a one-parent family adversely affects children's well-being. In Chapter 2 we argued that having only one parent in the household might affect children's motivation and work habits. The fact that differences in schooling and work persist even among children with similar levels of ability lends support to this hypothesis.

As a final check on the link between family structure and future employment prospects, we looked at reports of idleness among young men in the NLSY sample in 1988 when they were between the ages of twenty-three and twenty-six. Again, we found that young men from disrupted families were more likely to be idle or inactive than young men from two-parent families. The fact that the relationship between family structure and inactivity persists into the midtwenties is an indication that our previous results are not

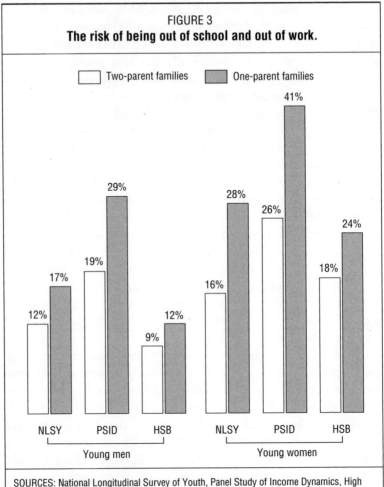

**FIGURE 3**
**The risk of being out of school and out of work.**

SOURCES: National Longitudinal Survey of Youth, Panel Study of Income Dynamics, High School and Beyond Study.
NOTE: One-parent families include stepfamilies. All numbers are adjusted for race, sex, mother's education, father's education, number of siblings, and place of residence. All differences from two-parent families are statistically significant.

just picking up a temporary phenomenon. Instead, it appears that growing up with only one parent has a lingering effect on young men's chances of finding and keeping a job.[8]

Having only one parent in the household also increases the risk of idleness among young women, especially those who are mothers. It would not be accurate to call young mothers "idle," since childrearing is generally accepted as a socially responsible activity. But if we consider the opportunity costs to young women of *not* investing in school or work, it is hard to ignore the fact that these young mothers are going to have a harder time down the road than their peers who did not become mothers during their teens.

Even when we exclude those with children, young women have higher rates of idleness than young men. We suspect that this is due to continuing differences in cultural expectations for young men and women. Young women are nearly as likely to be in the labor force as young men, but the pressure to become financially independent is probably greater for young men (once they have stopped school) than it is for young women. This means that young women have a little more time to search for a job, to change jobs, and to move in and out of the labor force than young men have. For all these reasons we would expect to find a higher percentage of young women idle or inactive at any point in time, and indeed that is what the data in Figure 3 show.

## EARLY FAMILY FORMATION

The last set of indicators we will examine closely compares adolescents according to their family formation behavior. Here we look at early marriage as well as early childbirth, both marital and nonmarital. As we noted in Chapter 2, early family formation is a fairly good predictor of a young woman's earning potential, and it also tells us a good deal about her future family obligations. Adolescent girls who become mothers are less likely to obtain a high school diploma and less likely to gain on-the-job training than adolescents who delay childbearing. They are also more likely to become single mothers and all that this entails.

## Early Childbearing

Approximately 20 percent of the women in our samples became mothers before reaching age twenty. This figure is nearly identical to the percentage who failed to obtain a high school diploma. The two indicators are highly correlated, although the relationship is not perfect. Nearly 70 percent of the young mothers in our samples eventually obtained a diploma, compared with over 90 percent of the young women who did not have a child by age twenty. If we count only high school diplomas, and exclude GEDs, we see that only 55 percent of the young mothers finished high school on time.

Women born in the 1940s and early 1950s were more likely to become teen mothers than women born after 1952, and they were more likely to be married at the time their first child was born. Of the women in our sample who were born between 1943 and 1952 and who became teen mothers during the 1950s and early sixties, approximately 75 percent were married when they gave birth. Of those who were born between 1953 and 1967 and who became teen mothers during the 1970s and 1980s, about 50 percent were married when their child was born.

Figure 4 compares the fertility experiences of young women from two-parent and one-parent families. Each bar is divided into two segments: the lower segment shows the proportion of young women who had a marital birth, and the upper segment shows the proportion who had a birth outside marriage. Together, the two segments show the percentage of women who became teen mothers (as represented by the number at the top of the bar).

Growing up in a disrupted family increases the risk of becoming a teen mother by a substantial amount. This is true regardless of whether we look at marital or nonmarital childbearing. The increase ranges from a low of 5 percentage points in the HSB data to a high of 17 percentage points in the PSID.[9]

The relationship between family structure and early childbearing is weaker in the HSB data than in the other surveys, probably because young women who drop out of school before their sophomore year are not included in these data. If teen mothers (or those who become teen mothers) in one-parent families are more likely

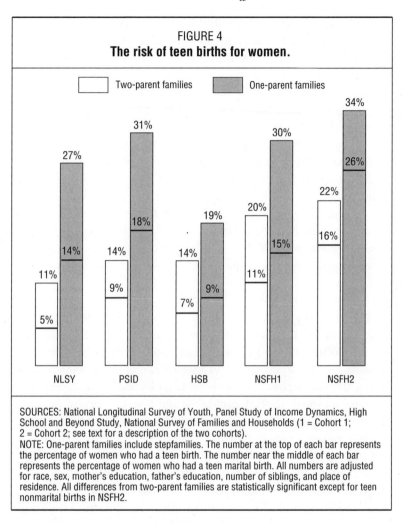

FIGURE 4
**The risk of teen births for women.**

☐ Two-parent families    ▨ One-parent families

SOURCES: National Longitudinal Survey of Youth, Panel Study of Income Dynamics, High School and Beyond Study, National Survey of Families and Households (1 = Cohort 1; 2 = Cohort 2; see text for a description of the two cohorts).
NOTE: One-parent families include stepfamilies. The number at the top of each bar represents the percentage of women who had a teen birth. The number near the middle of each bar represents the percentage of women who had a teen marital birth. All numbers are adjusted for race, sex, mother's education, father's education, number of siblings, and place of residence. All differences from two-parent families are statistically significant except for teen nonmarital births in NSFH2.

to drop out of school prematurely than their counterparts in two-parent families, we would expect to find a smaller family-structure effect in a school-based survey.

Living with a single parent has no discernible effect on the risk of a nonmarital teen birth for women born in the 1940s and early 1950s (NSFH, Cohort 2). But for those women born after 1953, it nearly doubles the risk (NSFH, Cohort 1). The effect of family structure on nonmarital childbearing appears to be a fairly recent phenomenon in the United States. This could be due in part to changes in the marital status of single mothers. Widowed mothers were much more common in the early cohort, whereas never-married mothers were more common in the later cohort.

It could also be due to changing social norms. During the 1950s, when out-of-wedlock childbearing was highly stigmatized, young women tried hard to avoid a nonmarital birth regardless of their family situation. If they became pregnant, they usually married the father before their child was born. After the sexual revolution in the early 1960s, young men and women felt less pressure to marry, even if the girl became pregnant. It is likely that the daughters of single mothers were leaders in this respect, since they had a better understanding of how single mothers cope with their situation.

### Early Marriage among Young Women

What about early marriage not involving children? Are young women from disrupted families more likely to marry in their teens than young women raised in two-parent families? It is not clear that an early marriage reduces future well-being; it may provide some young women with an incentive to forgo leisure activities and invest in human capital. Even if marriage itself is not a barrier, however, the fact that early marriage is related to early childbearing and divorce makes it a good predictor of possible problems in the future.

Looking at early marriage can provide us with additional information about the mechanisms underlying the link between family structure and early childbearing. Both marriage and motherhood mark the formation of a new family—the transition from the family of origin to the family of procreation. If daughters from one-parent families are motivated to start their families early because of a desire to leave home and find a mate, we would expect family structure to be related to early marriage just as it is related to early childbearing.

Except for the HSB, the data showed that family disruption did not increase the likelihood of marriage (see Appendix C). Thus it does not appear that young women from one-parent families are more motivated to find a husband than young women from two-parent families.

A potential problem with our results is that they fail to identify young women who are cohabiting, a status that has become increasingly common among young men and women. It is possible that young women from one-parent families are leaving home and forming unions earlier than young women from two-parent families but we are not picking this up with our data, which ignore cohabitation.

There is some support for this hypothesis. Arland Thornton, in his longitudinal study of mothers and daughters in the Detroit area, found that family disruption increased the likelihood of cohabitation but not marriage for young white women. Kathleen Kiernan's research on young men and women in the United Kingdom shows that adolescents from one-parent families leave home earlier than those from two-parent families.[10]

## Early Family Formation among Young Men

Early family formation is more closely related to women's future well-being than to men's. It is also much more common among young women. Nonetheless, it is useful to ask whether family structure affects both sexes the same way. We looked at the experiences of the young men in our samples with respect to teen marriage without children, teen fatherhood within marriage, and teen fatherhood outside marriage. From past research we know that men who do not marry the mothers of their children are reluctant to acknowledge their paternity, and therefore the findings regarding unmarried fatherhood, as reported by young men, should be viewed with a bit of skepticism.

Early family formation is much less common among men than among women. Whereas about 20 percent of the women in our samples gave birth in their teens, and another 10 percent married and remained childless, only about 5 percent of the young men had married and remained childless, and only about 5 percent reported having a child before age twenty. In short, nearly 30 percent of the women had formed a new family by the time they were twenty, as compared with only 10 percent of the men. This is about what we would expect, since men begin their families about two years later than women, on average.

While family formation is much less common among teen men than women, the effects of family disruption are similar for the two sexes. Living in a one-parent family increases the likelihood of becoming a teenage father, according to the NLSY and PSID data. The HSB estimates show no effect of family structure on early fatherhood, whereas the NSFH Cohort 1 data show a large effect on nonmarital births (see Appendix C).

## SEX, RACE, AND EDUCATION DIFFERENCES

Thus far, we have looked at how family disruption affects the average child. Yet many people want to know how family disruption affects particular subgroups in the population. They want to know which groups suffer the most and which ones suffer the least, and they want to know how their own children would fare in the event of a divorce or nonmarital birth.

To address these questions, we calculated predicted probabilities of dropping out of high school for young men and women separately, and we calculated predicted probabilities for dropping out of high school, being idle, and becoming a teen mother for children from different racial and social backgrounds.

Much of the early theorizing about "fatherless families" was derived from psychoanalytic theory, which emphasized the importance of fathers and male role models in the psychosexual development of boys. Indeed, the early empirical research on single parenthood often focused exclusively on boys. We now know that fathers play an important role in daughters' development, too. And recent empirical work suggests that divorce is just as harmful for girls as for boys, although the consequences are often manifested in different ways. Boys tend to express their feelings by acting out, whereas girls tend to hold their feelings inside.

In terms of high school achievement, our data show that young women are just as adversely affected by family disruption as young men (see Appendix C). Indeed, living with only one parent may have a more negative effect on girls than on boys. The NLSY survey shows an 18 percentage point difference in dropout rates for girls in one- and two-parent families, whereas it shows only a 15 percentage point difference for boys. The PSID indicates an 11 percentage point difference for girls and a 7 percentage point difference for boys. The other two surveys do not detect a sex difference in the effect of family disruption on high school dropout rates, which should make us cautious about interpreting these results.

What about race and ethnic differences? Are white children more or less affected by family disruption than black and Hispanic children? Since whites are more common than other racial and ethnic groups, the effects of family disruption on the average white child are very similar to the effects on children as a whole. Living with only one parent increases the probability of dropping out of high school for the average white child by 17 percentage points (Table 2); it increases the probability of becoming a teen mother by 14 percentage points (for the average young white woman); and it increases the probability of being idle by only 3 percentage points (for the average young white man).

Black and Hispanic children come from less advantaged backgrounds than white children, and their underlying risk of dropping out of school (or experiencing one of the other events) is greater than that of whites to begin with. Thus, we might expect the absolute effect of family disruption to be greater on blacks and Hispanics than on whites. On the other hand, since single motherhood is more common and perhaps better institutionalized in the black and Hispanic communities,[11] we might expect the proportionate effect of family disruption on minority children to be smaller than the proportionate effect on white children.

With respect to school success, several important points can be made about racial differences in the effects of family structure (Table 2). First, family disruption is clearly not the only cause of dropping out of school for children of any racial background. A substantial proportion of children from two-parent families of all racial and ethnic groups fail to graduate from high school. Second, the *proportionate increase in risk* associated with family disruption is much smaller for blacks and Hispanics than for whites. Family

## TABLE 2
### Racial, ethnic, and educational differences in the effect of family disruption on children.

| Child background | High school dropout risk | | Teen birth risk (women) | | Idleness risk (men) | |
|---|---|---|---|---|---|---|
| | Two-parent families | One-parent families | Two-parent families | One-parent families | Two-parent families | One-parent families |
| **Average child** | | | | | | |
| White | 11% | 28% | 8% | 22% | 10% | 13% |
| Black | 17 | 30 | 26 | 40 | 21 | 30 |
| Hispanic | 25 | 49 | 24 | 46 | 20 | 20 |
| **Advantaged child** | | | | | | |
| White | 5 | 16 | 1 | 5 | 5 | 6 |
| Black | 4 | 8 | 6 | 11 | 9 | 14 |
| Hispanic | NA | NA | NA | NA | NA | NA |
| **Disadvantaged child** | | | | | | |
| White | 24 | 51 | 19 | 44 | 19 | 24 |
| Black | 23 | 40 | 29 | 45 | 24 | 33 |
| Hispanic | 29 | 53 | 24 | 46 | 19 | 19 |

*Source:* National Longitudinal Survey of Youth.

*Note:* One-parent families include stepfamilies. An advantaged child is defined as a child whose two parents have some college education. A disadvantaged child is defined as a child whose two parents have less than a high school degree. All numbers are adjusted for race, mother's education, father's education, number of siblings, and place of residence. NA = sample size too small to estimate.

disruption increases the chances of school failure by a factor of 2.5 for the average white child, 2.0 for the average Hispanic child, and 1.8 for the average black child.

Finally, the dropout rate for the average white child from a disrupted family is *higher* than the dropout rate for the average black or Hispanic child from a two-parent family. The white-black comparison in dropout rates is especially striking. White children from disrupted families have a much higher dropout rate than black children from two-parent families, and they have virtually identical dropout rates to those of black children from disrupted families (28 versus 30). This last contrast underscores the importance of family disruption for white children's school success and helps place it in perspective. *For the average white child, family disruption eliminates the advantage of being white with respect to high school graduation.*

The pattern for teen motherhood is similar to the pattern for dropping out of high school, although not as striking. Family disruption is not the only cause of teen motherhood, but it does increase the probability that a young woman will become a teen mother. The proportionate increase in risk is greatest among whites, followed by Hispanics and then blacks, as was true for high school dropout rates. Even so, young white women have a lower probability of becoming teen mothers than young black and Hispanic women, regardless of whether they live with two parents or one.

The pattern for idleness is different from the patterns for high school dropout and teen motherhood. In this particular instance, black children are the most negatively affected by family disruption.

Middle-class and upper-middle-class parents want to know how much their children will suffer from a divorce. To answer this question, we calculated probabilities for children from "advantaged families," defined as families in which both the mother and father had attended college. Fifteen percent of the white children in our sample fell into this category, as did 4 percent of black children. The percentage of Hispanic children who met this criterion was less than 1 percent—too small a group to analyze.

Children from advantaged families have much lower dropout rates and are much less likely to be idle or to be teen mothers than the average child (Table 2). Among white children whose parents have some college education, idleness and early childbirth are relatively rare regardless of family structure. Family disruption has virtually no effect on idleness. The differences suggest that white parents with some college education need not worry too much about their sons becoming idle.

In contrast, white middle-class parents do need to worry about the effects of family disruption on their daughters' chances of becoming a teen mother and their children's school performance. The chances that a white girl from an advantaged background will become a teen mother is five times as high, and the chances a white child will drop out of high school is three times as high if the parents do not live together. Moreover, dropping out of high school is likely to be only the tip of the iceberg. For every child who actually drops out of school as a result of family disruption, there are likely to be three or four more whose performance is affected even though they manage to graduate.

White middle-class parents also need to worry about their child's college performance. The likelihood of graduating from college for white children from advantaged backgrounds is about 9 percentage points lower among children from disrupted families than among children from two-parent families, and this number disguises what is actually a large sex difference in the effect of family disruption. *Young white women from disrupted advantaged families are 12 percentage points less likely to graduate from college than their peers who live with both parents.* In contrast, young white men from disrupted advantaged families are only 4 percentage points less likely to graduate. The sex difference in college graduation is in addition to the sex difference in high school graduation that we reported earlier for the NLSY data, since we only examine college graduation for young people who finished high school. Again, the sex difference in college graduation is limited to one data set—the NLSY—and therefore we are not as confident of this effect as we are of some of the other results.

Black middle-class parents who break up may feel comforted to know that their children are likely to finish high school regardless of whether their parents live together or apart (although a disruption increases the risk by a factor of two). But even more than white middle-class parents, they do need to worry about college performance. Black children from advantaged two-parent families have a 37 percent chance of graduating from college, whereas black children from advantaged disrupted families have a 29 percent chance of graduating.

To examine how children from disadvantaged backgrounds are affected by family disruption, we selected children whose mothers and fathers had not graduated from high school. Only 16 percent of white children fell into this category, whereas 27 percent of black children and 50 percent of Hispanic children fit this description.

The future success of children of low-educated parents is rather bleak, regardless of whether they live with two parents or with one or neither parent. High school dropout rates, teen motherhood rates, and idleness rates are between 20 and 30 percent even among children from two-parent families (see Table 2). For those who live in disrupted families, the risk of dropping out of high school and becoming a teen mother is between 1.5 and 2 times as great. This translates into a very large absolute effect because the underlying risk is very high to begin with. Thus, the probability of dropping out of high school or becoming a teen mother goes up by about 27 percentage points for a white child who is from a disadvantaged background with an absent parent.

Again, it is worth noting that the consequences of family disruption are *smaller* for disadvantaged black and Hispanic children than for disadvantaged white children, both in terms of percentage points and in terms of proportionate effects. White children from disadvantaged backgrounds and disrupted families look very similar to black and Hispanic children in those categories in terms of their risk of teen motherhood, and they look substantially worse than black children in terms of their risk of high school failure.

## CONCLUSION

Children who grow up apart from a parent are disadvantaged in many ways relative to children who grow up with both parents. They are less likely to graduate from high school and college, they are more likely to become teen mothers, and they are somewhat more likely to be idle in young adulthood. The differences between children from two-parent and disrupted families are not overwhelming and not inevitable, but they are large enough to merit our concern. The average young woman from a white one-parent family has about the same risk of becoming a teen mother as the average black or Hispanic young woman from a two-parent family, and she is more likely to drop out of school than the average black child.

In short, some of the advantages associated with being white are equivalent to the advantages associated with living with two parents. The only measure of success that does not fit the general pattern is idleness. Family structure is only weakly related to idleness among whites and not related at all among Hispanics. But among young black men, family structure has a substantial effect on their chances of finding steady work.

Given what we know about the labor market problems of young black men, we should not be too surprised to learn that family structure has a larger effect on their behavior than on young men from other racial and ethnic groups. Whereas all children have more or less equal access to a high school education and to information about birth control, young black men are more disadvantaged than young white or Hispanic men when it comes to finding and keeping a job. They live in communities with higher concentrations of poverty and unemployment, and they experience more discrimination than other young men.[12]

Even children from advantaged families are vulnerable to the negative effects of family disruption. Among whites, living in a one-parent family takes away some of the advantages of having parents with a college education; it puts white middle-class children on a par with white children whose parents have never been to college but have remained together. This is not the case for blacks. Black children from advantaged families whose parents split up do much better than black children in general. But when we compare advantaged black families to one another, we find that two-parent families are more likely to graduate a child from high school and college than are one-parent families.

Finally, girls may be more adversely affected than boys by family disruption. There is some evidence that the effect of living with one parent on dropping out of high school is greater for young women than young men, and there is also evidence that the effect of family disruption on college graduation is greater for young women than young men. These findings are not consistent across all four surveys, however, and therefore should be viewed as tentative.

# CHAPTER FOUR

# WHAT
# HURTS AND
# WHAT HELPS

In Chapter 3 we treated all children from disrupted families as though they were alike. Children born to unmarried mothers were combined with children who lived with divorced mothers and widowed mothers. Children who experienced single parenthood in early childhood were combined with children whose parents divorced in adolescence. And the presence of other adults in the household—grandmothers, cohabiting men, and stepfathers—was ignored. In this chapter we ask whether any of these factors make a difference to the well-being of children.

The answer to this question should be useful to parents as well as policymakers who may be in a position to influence the conditions under which children experience single parenthood, even if they cannot prevent it. If the effect of living apart from a parent is the same for children of never-married parents as it is for children of divorced parents, for example, we should be less concerned about whether or not the parents are married when the child is born. We would care about whether or not an unmarried father supported his child after birth, just as we care about whether or not a divorced father supports his child, but we would be less concerned about the parents' marital status at birth. This is a very important point since much of the recent discussion of the potentially negative consequences of single parenthood focuses on out-of-wedlock childbirth as opposed to divorce. Judging from the comments in the popular media, many people seem to believe that single parenthood due to nonmarital childbearing is a serious social problem, whereas single parenthood due to divorce and separation is not.

Similarly, if remarriage reduces the negative consequences of single parenthood, or if having a grandmother in the household improves children's well-being, we might encourage divorced and widowed mothers to remarry (or, in the case of unwed mothers, to marry someone other than the biological father) or to live in multigenerational households. Again, many commentators talk as though having a stepfather or a grandparent in the household will solve the problems associated with single motherhood, and some states have even passed laws to encourage single mothers on welfare to remarry or to live with their own parents.

## DOES THE CAUSE OF INSTABILITY MATTER?

Policymakers and the public in general have expressed special concern for children born to unmarried mothers. Part of this is due to the fact that many people disapprove of out-of-wedlock childbearing for religious reasons. Part may be traced to the fact that unwed mothers have a high risk of poverty and welfare dependence. The latter causes concern not only because of the costs to taxpayers but because many people fear that our current welfare system encourages single motherhood. While the evidence suggests that welfare benefits have only a small effect on out-of-wedlock childbearing,[1] unmarried mothers are the fastest growing segment of the single-mother population, and therefore they merit special attention. In 1970 approximately 7 percent of all children living with one parent were living with a never-married parent; by 1990 the number was 31 percent.[2]

Given the rapid increase in the proportion of all children being born to unmarried mothers, it is sensible to ask whether or not these children are doing less well than children of divorced and separated mothers or widowed mothers. There are several reasons for thinking that the answer might be yes. Because unmarried mothers are younger and much more likely to be poor than other single mothers—64 percent of the former versus 37 percent of the latter—they are likely to experience more stress and economic insecurity.[3] For this reason alone, we would expect the children in these families to do less well in school. Alternatively, children whose parents divorce may experience more parental conflict than children of unmarried parents, and their reaction to "father loss" may be greater, since they had shared a household with their fathers and may have become more attached.

We might expect children of widowed mothers to do better than children of other single mothers for a number of reasons. First, the death of a parent usually involves fewer changes overall than the loss of a parent through separation or divorce. Widowed mothers as a group are more financially secure than other single mothers, and therefore they are less likely to change employment or residence after the father is gone. Nor is parental conflict an issue for these children.

To determine whether the cause of single parenthood makes a difference for children who grow up with only one parent, we divided children from disrupted families into three groups: those born to unmarried parents, those with divorced and separated parents, and those with a widowed parent. Figure 5 reports the risk of dropping out of high school and becoming a teen mother for these three groups of children. (The NSFH collected data on employment histories, but we were concerned about whether respondents could remember accurately so far back in time, and therefore we decided not to use the idleness information in these data. Teen childbearing and high school graduation are much easier to recall than employment, and the information is more likely to be reliable. The data reported throughout this chapter are based on Cohort 1 of the NSFH and are adjusted for differences in family background.) In this chapter, dropping out of high school is defined as not receiving a high school diploma, as opposed to not receiving a diploma or a GED. We chose this indicator because it is more sensitive to differences among children from disrupted families and because it may be a more reliable indicator of school success than the combination of diploma and GED.

Children born to an unmarried mother are 6 percentage points

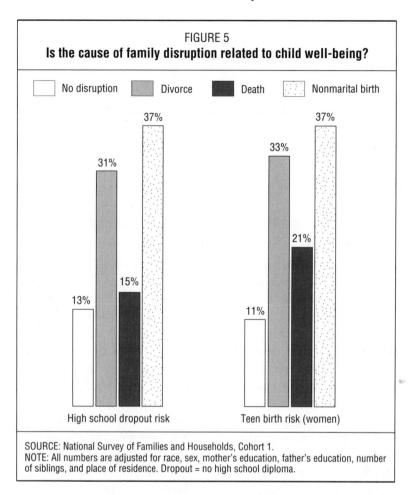

FIGURE 5
**Is the cause of family disruption related to child well-being?**

☐ No disruption  ▨ Divorce  ■ Death  ⬚ Nonmarital birth

SOURCE: National Survey of Families and Households, Cohort 1.
NOTE: All numbers are adjusted for race, sex, mother's education, father's education, number of siblings, and place of residence. Dropout = no high school diploma.

more likely to drop out of high school than children whose parents divorce. The difference is statistically significant but not very large. Children who lose a parent through death, however, have a *much* lower dropout rate than other children from disrupted families. The risk of dropping out of high school is the same for children who live with a widowed parent as for children who live with both their parents—15 and 13 percent, respectively, a difference that is not statistically significant.

A similar pattern appears when we look at teenage motherhood. Young women who were born out of wedlock have a slightly higher chance of becoming a teen mother as young women whose parents divorced (the 4 percentage point difference is not statistically significant), whereas young women who experience the loss of a parent through death are much less likely to become teen mothers than young women who experience a divorce—21 percent for the former as compared with 33 percent for the latter. In this case, the difference between girls of widowed mothers and girls in two-parent families is statistically significant.

## DO TIMING AND DURATION OF SINGLE PARENTHOOD MATTER?

Children in one-parent families differ with respect to how old they were when their parents separated, which might be expected to affect adjustment to the separation. Freudian-influenced psychological theories have pointed to early childhood as a critical period with long-term consequences for mental and emotional well-being. Thus many people have come to believe that marital disruptions in early childhood are worse than disruptions in middle childhood or adolescence. More recent extensions in developmental theory, however, along with new empirical work on the effects of divorce, have raised doubts about the unique importance of early childhood.

This work suggests that disruptions occurring in adolescence may be even more harmful than disruptions occurring in early childhood. Adolescence is a time when children need a great deal of parental supervision and emotional support, and it is a time when impulsive behavior has far-reaching consequences. Whereas young children may act out their anger over their parents' divorce by getting into fights with their friends or siblings, adolescents may act out by becoming sexually active and not using adequate birth control or by slacking off in school. While these different behaviors may reflect similar degrees of anger, the adolescent forms of acting out have more lasting negative consequences.

Children in single-parent families also differ with respect to how long they have lived with single mothers and how many disruptions in family structure they have experienced. In a case where parents divorce when a child is three years old and the mother remarries when the child is five, the child experiences two disruptions and lives with a single parent for two years, assuming no further disruptions. In another case where parents divorce when the child is five and the mother never remarries, the child experiences one disruption and lives with a single parent for thirteen years (up until age eighteen). In yet another case a mother may cohabit with a man, or several men in series, before remarrying. Which of these children is more disadvantaged? Are multiple changes more harmful to children, or are long periods of exposure to single motherhood the damaging factor? Theorists disagree about these matters and therefore it is hard to predict, a priori, which child will be more adversely affected.

Table 3 reports high school dropout rates and teen birth rates according to the age at which a child first experienced the loss of a parent, the length of time he or she lived with a single mother, the total number of family disruptions, and whether the mother remarried. Again, all of the estimates are adjusted for differences in family background characteristics. According to our findings, the age of the child at the time of the family disruption is not related to the risk of dropping out of school or early childbearing. Children who experience family disruption before they are five years old have about the same chance of dropping out of school and having a child before age twenty as children who experience a disruption during adolescence. The percentage differences are not statistically significant.

Moreover, the number of years of exposure to single parenthood does not seem to matter either. Children who live with a single mother for less than five years are about as successful as children who live with a single mother for more than five years. Even multiple changes in the family structure do not discriminate among children from one-parent families. Children who experience two or more disruptions due to divorces and remarriages have about the same risk of dropping out of school and having a teen birth as children who experience only one disruption.

---

### TABLE 3
### Do the timing and duration of family disruption make a difference in child well-being?

| Condition | High school dropout risk | Teen birth risk (women) |
|---|---|---|
| **Child's age at first disruption** | | |
| 0–5 | 33% | 35% |
| 6–11 | 29 | 30 |
| 12+ | 27 | 28 |
| | | |
| **Years in a one-parent family** | | |
| More than 5 | 29 | 30 |
| Fewer than 5 | 33 | 33 |
| | | |
| **Number of disruptions** | | |
| 1 or fewer | 31 | 33 |
| 2 or more | 32 | 33 |
| **Remarriage** | | |
| No | 31 | 30 |
| Yes | 30 | 33 |

*Source:* National Survey of Families and Households, Cohort 1.

*Note*: Sample includes only children from one-parent families. Estimates are based on separate models for each set of predictor variables: age at first disruption, years in a one-parent family, number of disruptions, remarriage. None of the differences are statistically significant.

---

A colleague, Roger Wojtkiewicz, has used both the NLSY and NSFH surveys to examine differences in children's family histories, and his findings are similar to our own. He finds that *exposure* to single parenthood, rather than timing, duration, or number of disruptions, is all that really matters for determining school achievement.[4] If a disruption occurs early, the yearly effect of living in a single-parent family is small; if it occurs late, the yearly effect is large. Either way, the bottom line is the same: living in a one-parent family reduces children's chances of graduating from high school, compared with children raised by two parents.

Two other colleagues—Lawrence Wu and Brian Martinson—have used the NSFH data to examine the relationship between family structure and premarital childbearing (not necessarily among teen mothers).[5] They find that the total number of disruptions is very important in predicting premarital childbearing, whereas living in a single-parent family or being born to an unmarried mother is not. Since they were looking at childbearing beyond age twenty and since they adjust for a different set of variables than we do—such as how early the child leaves home—the two analyses are not comparable. However, the fact that they find large effects associated with *changes* in family structure suggests that multiple disruptions may indeed be harmful to children.

## DO STEPPARENTS MAKE A DIFFERENCE?

Whether or not a mother remarries—or, in the case of an unwed mother, marries—is another factor that shapes children's experiences of family life. Larry Bumpass and James Sweet report that nearly half of all children who spend some part of their childhood with a single mother will eventually live for some period of time with a stepfather.[6] Nearly half of these new marriages will end in divorce before the child reaches eighteen. Thus, children whose mothers remarry when they are relatively young are likely to experience multiple disruptions in their family structure. What outcomes do we see among children who have lived with stepparents?

Table 3 compares children who live with a parent and stepparent with children who live with a single parent only. It shows that remarriage neither reduces nor improves a child's chances of graduating from high school or avoiding a teenage birth.

## DOES THE SEX OF THE PARENT MATTER?

Most children who live with only one parent live with their mothers, and we often equate single parenthood with single motherhood. Nevertheless, about 12 percent of children who live apart from a parent at age sixteen are living with their fathers. Thus it makes sense to ask whether children do better when they live with single fathers than with single mothers.

There are several reasons for thinking that fathers might make better single parents than mothers. Clearly, fathers have more income. If lack of economic resources is the key to why divorce has a negative effect on children, we might expect children in single-father families to do better than children in single-mother families. A father also provides a male role model, which may be especially important for boys. Finally, single fathers are more likely to be widowers than single mothers, and we have shown that widowhood is associated with better outcomes among children.

On the other hand, we might expect children in single-father families to be doing worse than children in single-mother families. Father custody is unusual in our society, and there is undoubtedly a good deal of selectivity associated with such an arrangement. If, for example, the father obtained custody because the mother is an alcoholic or is abusive, we would expect the child to do worse, not because of living with the father but because of the mother's problems. Women become single mothers for many reasons, including alcoholism or abuse on the part of the father, whereas men usually become single fathers when the mother is unwilling or unable to take care of the child. Despite the increase in joint custody and father custody, the average father still has a hard time gaining custody of his children unless he can prove that the mother is "unfit" or has a serious problem. Thus the average child in a single-father family is more likely to have a "problem nonresident parent" than is the average child in a single-mother family.

We found that single fathers do no better than single mothers at keeping their children in school. Dropout rates are nearly identical in the two types of families (Figure 6). Similarly, young women who live with single fathers are just as likely to become teen mothers as young women who live with single mothers. (The percentage point differences are not statistically significant.) The finding that children living with single fathers do as poorly with respect to schooling and early childbearing as children living with single mothers has been replicated with the NLSY and PSID surveys.

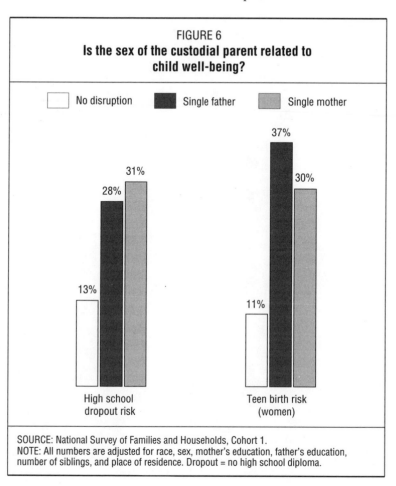

**FIGURE 6**
**Is the sex of the custodial parent related to child well-being?**

□ No disruption   ■ Single father   ▨ Single mother

High school dropout risk: 13% / 28% / 31%

Teen birth risk (women): 11% / 37% / 30%

SOURCE: National Survey of Families and Households, Cohort 1.
NOTE: All numbers are adjusted for race, sex, mother's education, father's education, number of siblings, and place of residence. Dropout = no high school diploma.

## DO GRANDMOTHERS HELP?

Grandmothers living with single mothers sometimes provide free childcare or contribute income to the family, both of which should make children better off. In addition, grandmothers may provide emotional support to the mother, which might improve the quality of the mother's parenting. They also may increase parental authority and control over the child. But is all this enough to offset the

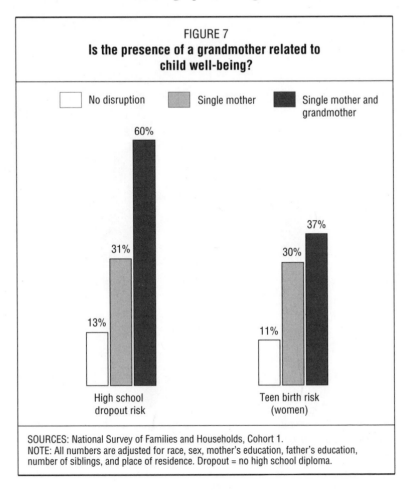

FIGURE 7
**Is the presence of a grandmother related to child well-being?**

No disruption    Single mother    Single mother and grandmother

High school dropout risk: 13%, 31%, 60%
Teen birth risk (women): 11%, 30%, 37%

SOURCES: National Survey of Families and Households, Cohort 1.
NOTE: All numbers are adjusted for race, sex, mother's education, father's education, number of siblings, and place of residence. Dropout = no high school diploma.

negative effects of single parenthood on school achievement and early childbearing?

Andrew Cherlin and Frank Furstenberg Jr. found that grandparents often help their adult children in times of crisis, such as divorce, and other researchers have shown that being raised by a mother and grandmother is just as good as being raised by two parents, at least in terms of children's psychological well-being.[7]

Most single mothers with adolescent children do not have a grandmother living in the household. Only 4 percent of the children in the NSFH data were living with a single mother and a grandmother when they were age sixteen, and this percentage was about the same in all of the surveys. The popular belief that grandmothers are helping single mothers raise their children probably arises from studies that focus on young teen mothers, many of whom live with their mothers or parents. Multigenerational households are relatively uncommon among older single mothers with adolescent children.

According to our data (Figure 7), having a grandmother in the home *increases* the risk of dropping out of high school and has virtually no effect on early childbearing. (The 7 percentage point difference is not statistically significant.) Young adults who live with a single mother and a grandmother are twice as likely to drop out of school as young adults who live with a single mother only.

There are a couple of reasons why the "grandmother effect" may be negative. First, we are looking at household composition when the child is sixteen, whereas studies that have found positive effects for grandmothers have usually looked at younger children. Having a grandmother in the family at age sixteen is quite unusual and may mean something very different from having a grandmother around at age three or age eight. For example, grandmothers may decide to live with a single mother and teenage child *because* the child is having trouble or because the mother is not doing a good job of parenting. Alternatively, a grandmother may be living in the household because she is disabled and needs someone to care for her. In either of these scenarios, we would not expect the relationship between grandmother co-residence and child well-being to be positive.

## ARE BOYS AND GIRLS AFFECTED DIFFERENTLY BY CIRCUMSTANCES?

In the previous chapter we noted that although there were many reasons for thinking that young men might be more negatively affected by family disruption than young women, the empirical evidence suggests that they are not. Indeed, there is some evidence that the opposite is true. In this chapter we look at whether the circumstances surrounding the disruption have different effects on boys and girls.

We were able to identify a couple of areas in which boys and girls respond differently. Being born to unmarried parents is more negative for boys than for girls, and the timing of the parents' divorce—whether it occurs in early childhood or in adolescence—is more important for girls than for boys. Girls who experience an early disruption (before age five) are much more likely to drop out of high school than girls who experience a late disruption (after age eleven). For boys, the age at which the disruption occurs does not matter. These findings are based on small samples and only one data set (the NSFH). Therefore we caution the reader against giving the results too much weight.

## ARE BLACK AND WHITE CHILDREN AFFECTED DIFFERENTLY BY CIRCUMSTANCES?

We also looked at whether blacks respond in the same way as whites to the conditions surrounding family disruption. Again, we found a couple of potentially important differences.

First, we found some evidence that living with a widowed mother was less beneficial for young black women than for young white women. Black girls who lost a parent through death were just as likely to become teen mothers as black girls who lost a parent through divorce or nonmarital birth. They were *more* likely to finish high school, however, which suggests that in some domains widowhood has similar effects for whites and blacks.

Second, living in a stepfamily at age sixteen was more advantageous for blacks than for whites. Young black men who lived in stepfamilies had a dropout rate of only 23 percent, which is comparable to the rate for blacks in two-parent families, and young black women in stepfamilies had the same risk of becoming a teen mother as young black women in two-parent families.

The finding that black children from stepfamilies do much better than black children from single-parent families can be interpreted in a couple of ways. On the one hand, if taken at face value, it could mean that stepfathers bring important economic and social resources to the family which enhance children's chances of success. Stepfathers not only increase family income, they also provide valuable role models and direct supervision. These resources may be even more important to young blacks than to young whites, since the former live in communities with fewer resources and less social control.

On the other hand, since remarriage is not very common among black single mothers (the ratio of single mothers to remarried mothers is 2 to 1), we cannot rule out the possibility that mothers who remarry are more advantaged to begin with, which might account for their children's higher success rate.

## SUMMARY

In this chapter we focused on children raised in one-parent families and asked whether the cause of the family's structure (widowhood, divorce, or being an unwed mother) or the age of the child at the time single parenthood began makes any difference in terms of the child's outcome. We found very little evidence that these differences matter. In general, compared with children living with both their parents, young people from disrupted families are more likely to drop out of high school, and young women from one-parent families are more likely to become teen mothers, irrespective of the conditions under which they began to live with single mothers and irrespective of whether their mothers remarry or experience subsequent disruptions.

But the exceptions to this rule are important and merit our attention. Children raised by widowed mothers do better in most dimensions than children raised by other single mothers. And boys born to unmarried mothers do worse than boys who live with divorced and separated mothers. Black children are more successful in school if they are born to married parents who live together, at least until the child reaches school age.

These different consequences associated with nonmarital birth and widowhood are worrisome because never-married mothers account for an increasing proportion of all single mothers, and widowed mothers account for a decreasing proportion. While it is certainly good that widowhood is on the decline, the fact that widowed mothers have more resources than other single mothers—in part because society treats them better—is an advantage that children will surely miss. If the results reported here are confirmed by other studies, and if they are picking up a true causal effect, this would suggest that the consequences of single parenthood for young black men's educational attainment will become more negative in the future.

On a more hopeful note, we found that having a stepfather in the household increases the likelihood of success among young black men and women. While this is good news insofar as it suggests that the negative consequences of family disruption may be attenuated by remarriage, we must not forget that the remarriage rate is low among blacks, and the proportion of black children who actually live with a stepfather is low. In the NSFH Cohort 1 sample, only about 33 percent of the young black men and women in one-parent families were living with a mother and stepfather, as compared with about half of white children. Even more important, the relationship between living in a stepfamily and higher educational achievement among black children may not be causal. Black single mothers who remarry are more advantaged before they remarry than other single mothers, and this could explain why their children are doing better in school.

Despite these caveats, we are struck by the overall similarities rather than the differences among children raised in different types of single-parent families. Our data lead us to conclude that the circumstances surrounding a family disruption are less critical to children's future well-being than the fact of the disruption itself.

# CHAPTER FIVE

# THE VALUE
# OF MONEY

Why are children who live apart from one of their parents more likely to drop out of school, become idle, and have a child before reaching age twenty than children who live with both parents? Is it because they have a lower standard of living? Is it because their parents provide less supervision or less emotional support? Or is it something about the neighborhoods they live in or the schools they attend? In the next three chapters, we will examine each of these possibilities and provide estimates of the degree to which they account for differences in well-being between children in two-parent and disrupted families.

Many people believe that poverty and economic insecurity are to blame for the lower achievement of children in single-parent families. Their suspicions would appear to be reasonable insofar as income is an important determinant of a person's life chances and future success, and insofar as single-parent families have less income overall than two-parent families.

The question of whether income differences can explain the disadvantages associated with single parenthood is of particular interest to policymakers, since income is a variable over which the government has some control. If differences in children's achievement are due entirely to differences in family income, it would be much easier to argue that the one-parent family is a viable family structure, lacking only in economic resources. The issue for policymakers would then be: Who should provide the additional economic support needed to compensate for the absence of a biological parent—society, the nonresident parent, a stepparent if one exists, or the mother?

Of course, the government is unlikely to ever fully compensate for the absence of a second parent. Taxpayers would object on the grounds that transferring money from married parents and childless taxpayers to parents who choose to maintain separate households is unfair. Nor can nonresident fathers be expected to fully compensate for the decline in the child's standard of living after a separation, since they too lose economies of scale. Nevertheless, much can be done to increase the economic resources of one-parent families, and the question of whether income is the major factor in accounting for the lower well-being of children in these families is a critical issue in the current policy debate.

Table 4 (top row) reports median family income in 1992 dollars for three types of families: two-parent families, single-parent families, and stepfamilies. (The numbers are not adjusted for differences in family background characteristics.) Two-parent families clearly have the most income, averaging over $60,000 per year. Stepfamilies are not far behind, with nearly $55,000 a year, and single-parent families have the least income, approximately $27,000 annually. The NLSY data showed a similar pattern, although the overall level of income was lower. Children who were living with both parents in 1979 had an average family income of $44,000, whereas children who were living with a single parent had an average income of $20,000, and children in stepfamilies had an income of $39,000. In both of these surveys, two-parent families have incomes that are more than twice as high as single-parent families. We would expect family income to be higher in the PSID because this survey asks many more questions about parents' income than does the NLSY (see Appendix A).

Some readers may be surprised at the high incomes of the families represented in Table 4. Even single-parent families appear to be doing well. This apparent anomaly is due to the fact that we are

TABLE 4

**Median income of two-parent families, single-parent families, and stepfamilies, by race and by mother's education (in 1992 dollars).**

| Race and education | Two-parent families | Single-parent families | Stepfamilies |
|---|---|---|---|
| All families | $61,135 | $27,065 | $54,594 |
| Whites | $63,270 | $31,349 | $55,360 |
| Blacks | $39,061 | $20,105 | $49,692 |
| Less than a high school degree | $43,693 | $22,305 | $39,234 |
| High school degree only | $63,071 | $30,297 | $57,945 |
| Some college education | $83,748 | $37,745 | $71,220 |

*Source:* Panel Study of Income Dynamics.
*Note:* Income measured at age 16.

looking at families with at least one adolescent child, which means that we are looking at families at or near the peak of parents' earning power. If we looked at all families with children under eighteen, the story would be different. In 1992 the median income was about $43,000 for all families with children, and it was about $13,500 for all single-parent families. The much lower income of all single-parent families, as compared with single-parent families with an adolescent child, highlights the fact that single parents are younger, on average, than married parents. This difference in parents' age must be kept in mind when examining income data on one-parent and two-parent families.

To get a better idea of differences in economic resources at the bottom end of the income distribution and to adjust for overall difference in family size, we contrast the poverty rates of children in two-parent families, single-parent families, and stepfamilies. The

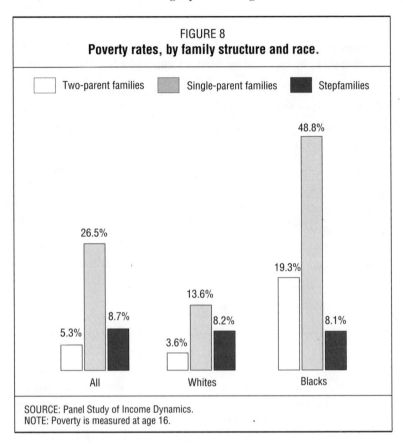

FIGURE 8
**Poverty rates, by family structure and race.**

☐ Two-parent families ▨ Single-parent families ■ Stepfamilies

48.8%

26.5%

8.7%

5.3%

13.6%

8.2%

3.6%

19.3%

8.1%

All    Whites    Blacks

SOURCE: Panel Study of Income Dynamics.
NOTE: Poverty is measured at age 16.

poverty threshold set by the U.S. Census Bureau in 1992 was $14,812 for a family of four and $11,973 for a single mother and two children.[1]

In general, the contrasts in poverty status, as shown in Figure 8, are consistent with the numbers in Table 4. Single-parent families have the highest poverty rates (26.5 percent), and two-parent families have the lowest rates (5.3 percent).

Stepfamilies are closer to the rates of two-parent families (8.7 percent). Again, the poverty rates of these families may strike the reader as unusually low, especially those of single-parent families.

Didn't we say in Chapter 2 that nearly half of all children in single-parent families were living below the poverty line? The answer to this question is the same as the answer to the question about income: when we look at families with an adolescent child, we are looking at families at the peak of their earning capacity. The poverty rate for all married-couple families (two-parent or step-families) was 8.4 in 1992, and the poverty rate for all single-parent families was 45.7.

Income is only one measure of economic status, however. Assets are another. The PSID has information on ownership of a home and car, which are the more common assets. Single-parent families are much less likely to own their own home and less likely to own a car than are two-parent families. Ninety-eight percent of the two-parent families in our data owned a car, and 87 percent owned their own home. In contrast, only 50 percent of single mothers owned their home, and only 70 percent owned a car. Stepfamilies looked similar to two-parent families in terms of car and home ownership. Ninety-seven percent owned a car, and 80 percent owned their own home. As before, in thinking about these numbers, the reader should keep in mind the fact that we are looking at families with an adolescent child, as opposed to families with only young children.

## RACE AND EDUCATION DIFFERENCES IN INCOME

The numbers reported thus far could simply be reflecting the fact that single-parent families overrepresent minorities and people with lower social class backgrounds. In order to determine whether the economic disparity between two-parent and one-parent families exists within racial and ethnic groups and within different social class backgrounds as well as for the population as a whole, we compare the family income and poverty rates of white and black families and of families with different educational backgrounds. Education groups are based on whether the mother had less than a high school degree, a high school degree only, or more than a high school degree.

Clearly the income difference between two-parent and one-

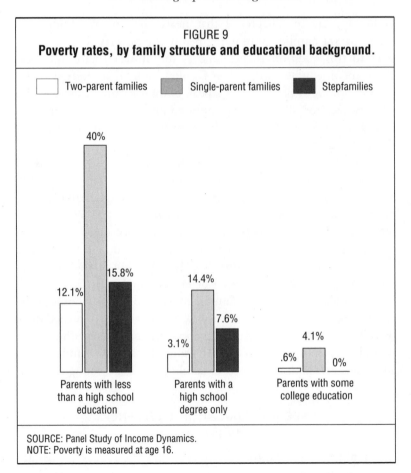

FIGURE 9
**Poverty rates, by family structure and educational background.**

☐ Two-parent families   ▨ Single-parent families   ■ Stepfamilies

40%

15.8%

12.1%

14.4%

7.6%

3.1%

4.1%

.6%   0%

Parents with less
than a high school
education

Parents with a
high school
degree only

Parents with some
college education

SOURCE: Panel Study of Income Dynamics.
NOTE: Poverty is measured at age 16.

parent families is not just a reflection of differences in race (Table 4). Black single mothers have about half the income of black mothers who are married. Notice that the family income of black stepfamilies is even higher than the family income of black two-parent families. These findings suggest that black single mothers do not remarry unless the income of their new partner is exceptionally high, and that those black women who do remarry are a very special group. Given these advantages, we would expect black children who grow up in stepfamilies to have lower dropout rates and teenage birth rates than black children who grow up with single mothers. Whatever disadvantages may arise from remarriage are more than made up for by the income advantage of these families.

A striking finding (evident in Figure 8) is the strong association between single parenthood and poverty among blacks. Nearly half of all black children who live in single-parent families are poor, as compared with only 20 percent of children in two-parent families. This is a huge difference—nearly 30 percentage points—and it demonstrates why the public is so concerned about black single mothers. Among whites, the differential in poverty rates is much smaller—13.6 percent for children living with single mothers versus 3.6 percent for children living with both parents.

The family structure contrast is even more stark when we compare children from different educational backgrounds (Figure 9). Single parenthood increases the chances of being poor by 28 percentage points among children of parents with less than a high school education and by less than 5 percentage points among children of parents with some college education.

In comparing racial differences in poverty rates by family structure, one must remember that poverty is not just a consequence of family disruption; it is also a cause. As we shall see in the next section, many black mothers have very low incomes prior to becoming single parents. It is also important to remember that black children in two-parent families have much higher poverty rates than white children in single-parent families. Hence, if there were no single-parent families, black children would still have much higher poverty rates than white children. This is partly because their parents have much less education, on average, than the parents of white children. It is also because black parents have lower earnings than white parents with similar levels of education.

## IS INCOME THE CAUSE OR THE EFFECT OF SINGLE PARENTHOOD?

Thus far, we have presented numbers that represent a snapshot of children's family life, taken when the child was age sixteen. These numbers do not tell us whether the association between divorce and family income is due to family dissolution itself or whether families that break up are less well off to begin with, and perhaps break up in part for that reason. To examine this issue of cause and effect more closely, we used the PSID to look at a subset of children who were living with both parents at age twelve.

We sorted these children into two groups: those whose parents stayed together and those whose parents separated or divorced by the time the child was seventeen. We then compared the income of these two groups at age twelve and again at age seventeen.[2]

We should point out that our approach exaggerates in some ways, and minimizes in others, the income loss associated with family disruption. By focusing on divorces and separations that occur during adolescence, we exaggerate the loss. Family income usually goes up as parents get older, and thus the income loss is potentially greater for families with adolescent children than for families with young children, simply because the former have more money to lose at the time of the divorce. Moreover, by restricting our sample to divorces and separations that occur after the child is twelve years old, we exclude children born to unmarried parents, a group for whom the income loss (or income foregone) is probably much smaller. Both of these restrictions exaggerate the size of the income drop.

On the other hand, by including in our sample mothers who remarried during the five years under scrutiny, we raise the average postdivorce income of the group, and thereby underestimate the average income loss caused by divorce. Unfortunately, the PSID sample is not large enough to allow us to examine separately families in which the mother remarries and families in which she remains single.

Family disruption during adolescence does lead to a substantial loss of income for children, regardless of the race and educational background of their parents (see note to Table 5). The average white adolescent whose parents divorce experiences a decline in family income of about $25,705, from $62,367 to $36,662. Notice that the income of adolescents in disrupted families is about $6,000 higher at age seventeen (Table 5) than the income of all children in single-parent families at age sixteen (Table 4), suggesting that

TABLE 5

**Median family income at ages twelve and seventeen for children in stable and unstable families, by race and by mothers' education (in 1992 dollars).**

| Race, education, and family type | Age 12 | Age 17 |
|---|---|---|
| **All** | | |
| Stable families | $59,741 | $64,789 |
| Unstable families | $55,864 | $33,509 |
| **Whites** | | |
| Stable families | $61,559 | $66,696 |
| Unstable families | $62,367 | $36,662 |
| **Blacks** | | |
| Stable families | $39,040 | $40,934 |
| Unstable families | $28,197 | $18,894 |
| **Less than high school education** | | |
| Stable families | $42,659 | $45,512 |
| Unstable families | $44,293 | $27,821 |
| **High school education** | | |
| Stable families | $61,858 | $65,798 |
| Unstable families | $60,725 | $37,290 |
| **Some college education** | | |
| Stable families | $80,191 | $91,766 |
| Unstable families | $73,833 | $38,082 |

*Source:* Panel Study of Income Dynamics.

*Note:* Stable families are defined as those in which the parents did not separate or divorce during the child's adolescence (ages 12–17); unstable families are defined as those in which the parents separated or divorced.

children who experience later disruptions come from more advantaged backgrounds than the average child from a disrupted family.

Notice that black two-parent families did not fare as well over the five-year period as white two-parent families. The average family income of white two-parent families went up by nearly $5,000, whereas the average income of black two-parent families went up by less than $2,000. These numbers reflect the differential effect on whites and blacks of the economic stagnation that took place during the 1970s and 1980s and lend support to the argument that economic difficulties often predate divorce and increase the risk of family disruption.[3]

## DO INCOME DIFFERENCES EXPLAIN
## DIFFERENCES IN CHILD WELL-BEING?

We have shown that living in a single-parent family is associated with less family income and higher poverty rates for children. We now ask whether income in adolescence *accounts for* any of the differences in child outcomes that we observed in Chapter 3. To answer this question, we focus on dropping out of high school, teen births, and idleness—and we compare children in different types of families before and after taking income into account.

Figure 10 reports our findings. The first bar shows the disadvantage (percentage point difference) associated with living in a single-parent family or stepfamily compared with a two-parent family *before* income is taken into account. The second bar shows the disadvantage after income is taken into account.

Notice that the differentials for each measure of child well-being are not identical to the differentials reported in Figures 1, 3, and 4 of Chapter 3. In Figure 1, for example, the difference in high school dropout was 10 percentage points for the PSID, whereas in Figure 10 it is only 6 percentage points for children from single-parent families and 10 percentage points for children from stepfamilies. The inconsistency between the two figures is due to two things: in the previous figure we combined children in single-parent and stepfamilies, whereas in Figure 10 we examine them separately; and in Figure 1 we included a small number of children who were not living with either parent at age sixteen, whereas here we include only children living with a single parent or a parent and a stepparent. The same applies for Figures 3 and 4.

The differences between children in single-parent families and stepfamilies should not be given very much weight since they are not statistically significant. Our main objective in separating the two groups of children is to get a better idea of the importance of

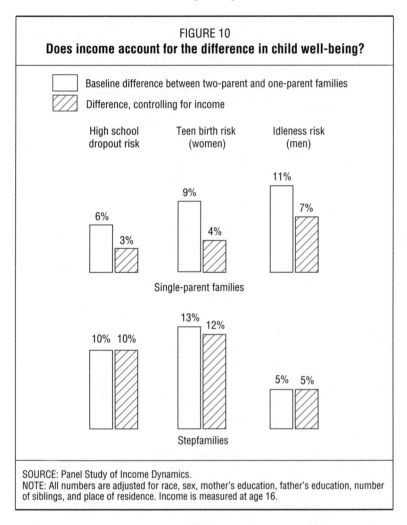

FIGURE 10
**Does income account for the difference in child well-being?**

☐ Baseline difference between two-parent and one-parent families

▨ Difference, controlling for income

| High school dropout risk | Teen birth risk (women) | Idleness risk (men) |

Single-parent families

6% 3%  9% 4%  11% 7%

| High school dropout risk | Teen birth risk (women) | Idleness risk (men) |

10% 10%  13% 12%  5% 5%

Stepfamilies

SOURCE: Panel Study of Income Dynamics.
NOTE: All numbers are adjusted for race, sex, mother's education, father's education, number of siblings, and place of residence. Income is measured at age 16.

income in "accounting" for differences between children in one-parent and two-parent families. Since stepfamilies have incomes that are very close to those of two-parent families, treating the two types of one-parent families together would mask the income effect.

We see that income accounts for a substantial portion of the risk of dropping out of high school between children in single-parent families and children in two-parent families. Before adjusting for income, the difference in graduation rates is 6 percentage points. After adjusting for income, the difference is only 3 percentage points. In contrast, income accounts for virtually none of the difference in dropout rates between children in stepfamilies and two-parent families. The difference in dropout rates is 10 percentage points before and after adjusting for differences in income. This is about what we would expect. As noted earlier, stepfamilies and two-parent families have very similar levels of income, and therefore income cannot explain differences in child well-being between these two types of families.

Looking at the figures for teen births, we see that income accounts for over half of the disadvantage associated with living in a single-parent family and for virtually none of the disadvantage associated with living in a stepfamily. The difference in the risk of a teen birth is 9 percentage points before adjusting for income and 4 percentage points after adjusting for income.

The pattern for idleness is similar, only in this case income accounts for about 36 percent of the difference (4 percentage points) between boys in two-parent families and boys in single-parent families.

We also used the NLSY to examine the importance of income, but here our findings were much less powerful than those from the PSID. Adjusting for income accounted for less than 15 percent of the differences between children in single-parent and two-parent families.

To obtain more information on income and to try to reconcile this discrepancy between surveys, we examined several other measures of educational attainment that were available in the NLSY, including test scores, college enrollment, and college graduation. When we used these other measures, as opposed to high school graduation, we found a pattern that was much more consistent with the PSID results. Income accounted for about 50 percent of the difference between children in single-parent and two-parent families in all three of these educational outcomes. Thus, while income does not do a very good job of explaining differences in high school graduation in the NLSY, it does appear to account for differences in other areas of educational attainment.

To further explore the importance of income in accounting for differences in school achievement between children from two-parent and single-parent families, we used a sample of families from the NSFH survey, and we looked at the relationship between family structure and three indicators of children's school success: whether or not the child was having "problems in school," how well the child was doing in school (for elementary and junior high children), and grade-point average (for high school children). In this analysis, all of the children were seventeen years old or less and the information was reported by a parent.

We found that family income accounted for about 40 percent of the the difference in grade-point average and school performance between children from two-parent and single-parent families. But income did not account for as much of the difference in behavioral problems between children from one-parent and two-parent families.

## DO CHANGES IN INCOME EXPLAIN
## CHILD WELL-BEING?

We have shown that the difference in income accounts for as much as half of the difference in school achievement and early childbearing of children in single-parent and two-parent families. While suggestive, this evidence is not sufficient to support the claim that declines in income following divorce are responsible for children's poorer performance in school. Since low income is a cause of family disruption as well as a consequence, it is possible that the "income effect" is due to predivorce differences in income rather than postdivorce differences.

In order to address this issue, we used the adolescent sample from the PSID which includes only children who were living with both parents at age twelve. We then estimated three equations: one looking at the effect of divorce on child well-being, holding constant family background characteristics (race, parents' education, number of siblings, and place of residence); a second looking at the effect of divorce on child well-being, holding constant family background characteristics *and predivorce income;* and a third looking at the effect of family instability on well-being, holding constant background characteristics, predivorce income, *and postdivorce income.*

Estimates from each of these equations are shown in Figure 11. The first bar represents the difference in high school dropout rates between children whose parents broke up and children whose parents stayed together, controlling for background characteristics. The second bar shows the difference in dropout rates, controlling for background factors plus family income at age twelve. And the third bar shows the difference in dropout rates, controlling for background factors plus income at ages eleven and seventeen.[4]

Again, the disadvantages associated with family disruption do not match exactly the disadvantages reported in Figure 10, although they come close. This is because Figure 11 is based on a different sample of children—children whose parents stayed together until the children were at least age twelve. The fact that the differentials are quite large in Figure 11 illustrates a point that we made earlier in Chapter 4: that disruptions in adolescence can be just as damaging to children as disruptions in early childhood or at birth.

Children whose parents break up during early adolescence are nearly 8 percentage points more likely to drop out of school than children whose parents stay together (first bar). This difference does not change when we adjust for predivorce income (second bar), which means that the difference in school completion is not due to differences in income prior to divorce. But when we adjust for both predivorce and postdivorce income (third bar), the gap in high school dropout falls by about 50 percent, from 8 to 4 percentage points.

This analysis confirms our previous estimates and makes us even more convinced that loss of income—or the lost resources for which income is a proxy—plays a major role in explaining why children in single-parent families have lower achievement than children in two-parent families.

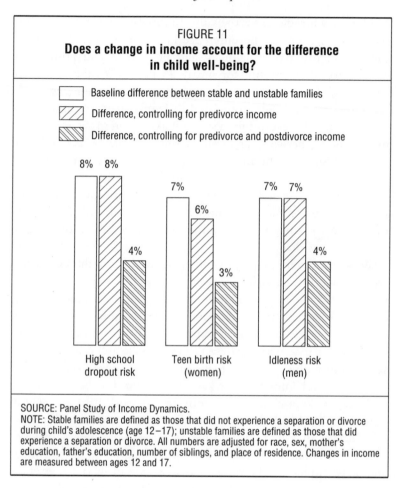

### FIGURE 11
### Does a change in income account for the difference in child well-being?

☐ Baseline difference between stable and unstable families

▨ Difference, controlling for predivorce income

▧ Difference, controlling for predivorce and postdivorce income

**High school dropout risk:** 8%, 8%, 4%

**Teen birth risk (women):** 7%, 6%, 3%

**Idleness risk (men):** 7%, 7%, 4%

SOURCE: Panel Study of Income Dynamics.
NOTE: Stable families are defined as those that did not experience a separation or divorce during child's adolescence (age 12–17); unstable families are defined as those that did experience a separation or divorce. All numbers are adjusted for race, sex, mother's education, father's education, number of siblings, and place of residence. Changes in income are measured between ages 12 and 17.

The pattern for teen birth is similar to the pattern for dropping out of high school. Adjusting for income differences prior to divorce accounts for very little of the difference in the risk of early childbearing between girls from two-parent and one-parent families (about 14 percent). Adjusting for both predivorce and postdivorce income, however, accounts for more than half of the difference in early childbearing.

The story for idleness is the same. In this case, predivorce income accounts for none of the difference between children from two-parent and one-parent families, and predivorce and postdivorce income together account for nearly 45 percent of the difference between children from two-parent and one-parent families.

Family income is closely related to family structure, and differences in income account for a substantial portion of the differences in well-being between children in single-parent and two-parent families. Moreover, the income effect is not simply a reflection of the fact that poor families are less likely to remain intact. These findings provide strong evidence that it is not just low income per se but the *loss* of economic resources associated with family disruption that is a major cause of the lower achievement of children whose parents divorce.

While we cannot pinpoint the specific mechanism through which income operates to raise or lower child well-being, in Chapter 2 we discussed several possible reasons. First, parents with more money can afford to send their children to better schools and they can afford to provide them with experiences like summer camps or extracurricular activities. These things increase a child's ability and satisfaction with school and make him or her more likely to value school. Second, knowing that parents can afford to help with college may make a child more motivated to work hard and stay in school. Finally, family income may affect the kind of neighborhood a child lives in. Children who live in middle-class neighborhoods where most children graduate from high school and go to college are likely to pick up the message that staying in school is essential and that "hanging out" or "dropping out" is not acceptable behavior within the community.

In contrast, loss of economic resources cannot explain why children in stepfamilies do worse than children from two-parent families. To answer this question—and to understand what, beyond loss of income, makes up the rest of the family-structure effect in single-parent families—we must consider in the next two chapters other areas of potential resource deprivation.

CHAPTER SIX

# THE ROLE OF PARENTING

In the last chapter we saw that while low income could explain as much as half of the disadvantage associated with living in a single-parent family, it was not an important factor in explaining the disadvantage associated with stepfamilies. In this chapter we focus on the role of parental resources and ask whether they can account for part of the lower achievement of children in disrupted families, particularly children in stepfamilies.

We have argued that besides economic security, children need parents who are willing to spend time with them reading, helping with homework, or just listening to how their day went at school. They also need parents who are willing and able to monitor and supervise their social activities outside school. As noted in Chapter 2, many children get off on the wrong track not because they lack talent or have the wrong values but because their opportunitites for getting into trouble are higher.

We suspect that parental involvement and supervision are weaker in one-parent families than in two-parent families. In one sense, this disadvantage is simply a matter of numbers: one parent has less time and less authority than two parents who can share responsibility and cooperate with each other. In another sense, however, it is due to the fact that single-parent families and stepfamilies are less stable in terms of personnel (grandmothers, mothers' boyfriends, and stepfathers are more likely to move in and out), which creates uncertainty about household rules and parental responsibility.[1]

## TIME WITH BIOLOGICAL FATHERS

About 24 percent of the children living with a divorced mother and about 33 percent of the children living with a never-married or remarried mother had no contact at all with their fathers during the past year, according to the NFSH data (Figure 12). In contrast, 30 percent of children living with a divorced mother, 38 percent of children living with a never-married mother, and 8 percent of children living in a stepfamily saw their fathers at least once a week. These numbers suggest that there is a good deal of diversity in father-child relationships in one-parent families.

Children living with never-married mothers are more likely than children of divorced mothers to *never* see their fathers—33 percent versus 24 percent. At the same time, they are slightly *more* likely to see their fathers on a weekly basis. This finding surprised us initially, since the conventional prejudice (masked as wisdom) suggests that most never-married mothers cannot even identify the father of their child. The numbers in Figure 12 suggest otherwise.[2]

How can we explain the fact that children living with never-married mothers are more likely to see their fathers once a week or more than are children of divorced mothers? At first we thought this rather surprising finding might have something to do with the age of the children. If the children of never-married mothers in our sample were substantially younger than the children of divorced mothers, they might see their fathers more often because less time had elapsed since their parents' breakup. We know that father-child contact declines rapidly during the first few years after a separation and so we reasoned that what we were observing might be a "recent-separation" effect.

To explore this possibility further, we restricted our sample to children under five. This makes the two groups of children—those living with never-married mothers and those with divorced mothers—more equal with respect to the amount of time their fathers

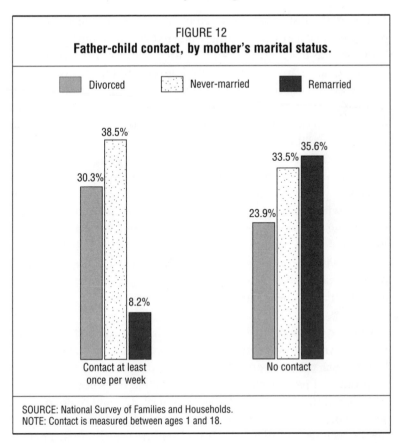

FIGURE 12
**Father-child contact, by mother's marital status.**

Divorced    Never-married    Remarried

**Contact at least once per week**
- Divorced: 30.3%
- Never-married: 38.5%
- Remarried: 8.2%

**No contact**
- Divorced: 23.9%
- Never-married: 33.5%
- Remarried: 35.6%

SOURCE: National Survey of Families and Households.
NOTE: Contact is measured between ages 1 and 18.

could have been absent. Indeed, it puts children of never-married mothers at a disadvantage since their parents' relationship is more likely to have ended at birth. Even with this more restricted sample, we found that children living with never-married mothers were more likely to see their fathers on a weekly basis than children of divorced single mothers. The similarity in the amount of contact between children and fathers leads us to believe that these two types of single-mother families—formerly married mothers and never-married mothers—are not as different as people have thought. Indeed, as family disruption and single parenthood have become more common, the distinction between children born inside and outside marriage has become increasingly blurred. About a third of children born outside marriage are born to formerly married women and about a quarter are born to cohabiting parents, about two thirds of whom eventually marry each other. In the next section we shall see that never-married single mothers are not very different from formerly married mothers when it comes to the time they spend with their children.

While children of never-married parents are as likely to have frequent contact with their fathers as the children of divorced and separated parents, what most people want to know is whether contact with the nonresident father makes any difference for child well-being. To date the evidence on this queston is mixed. Whereas studies based on small, convenience samples suggest that frequent contact with the nonresident father may help children adjust to divorce, studies based on large, nationally representative surveys indicate that frequent father contact has *no* detectable benefits for children.[3]

One explanation for why contact with a nonresident father may not be correlated with enhanced child well-being is that the benefits of contact depend on whether or not the parents get along with each other. If parents cooperate and the child does not feel torn in two directions, contact may be beneficial. If parents do not get along, contact may increase the parents' opportunity to express hostile feelings and thereby end up harming the children. There is some empirical evidence that this explains why the average effect of father contact is zero—the positive and negative effects of these two types of contact are canceling each other out.[4]

## TIME WITH MOTHERS

Children in one-parent families also spend less time with their mothers than children in two-parent families, although the loss of mother's time is not nearly as great as the loss of father's time. We compared mothers' involvement with children across several different types of families.[5] We asked how often (during the past week) the mother had breakfast and dinner with her child and how often she read to the child.

Single mothers and remarried mothers, we found, are less likely to share meals with their children (especially the dinner meal) than mothers in two-parent families (Table 6). The absolute difference in meal time is small—less than half a meal per week on average. But it is statistically significant, and small differences accumulate over time. Half a meal per week adds up to twenty-six meals a year.

Some readers may wonder whether the difference in meals is really important. If single mothers are sharing fewer meals with their children because the children are with the nonresident father, this would not mean that children were sharing fewer meals with their parents overall. Unfortunately, things don't seem to work this way. Children who have frequent contact with their nonresident fathers—at least once a week—actually share more meals with their mothers than children who spend less time with their fathers. It appears that some children have "involved parents" while others have "uninvolved parents."[6]

Divorced mothers appear to compensate for this deficit at mealtime by spending *more* time reading to their children. Indeed, never-married mothers also report reading to their children as often as married mothers. We should note that our estimates of the time mothers spend reading to their children are quite different from those reported in some previous studies. The economists Anne Hill and June O'Neill found that poor single mothers on welfare were much less likely to read to their children than divorced or married mothers. This possible discrepancy between our results and theirs could be due to the fact that the mothers in our sample are older than the mothers in their study. It could also be due to the fact that Hill and O'Neill distinguish between single mothers on welfare and other single mothers, whereas we do not. Alternatively, the discrepancy may reflect the fact that our information comes from mothers' reports, whereas theirs comes from a combination of mothers' reports and interviewer observations. We will have more to say about this in the next section when we look at children's reports of parental involvement.

## TABLE 6
### Mother's involvement and supervision.

| Mother's behavior (times per week) | Two-parent family | Mother and stepfather | Mother and partner | Divorced mother | Never-married mother |
|---|---|---|---|---|---|
| Breakfast with child | 3.68 | **2.80** | **2.84** | 3.50 | 3.55 |
| Dinner with child | 6.01 | **5.66** | **5.33** | **5.49** | **5.47** |
| Reading to child | 4.34 | 4.27 | 4.26 | **4.56** | 4.45 |
| Hugs/praises child | 3.69 | 3.69 | 3.63 | 3.72 | **3.58** |
| Scolds/spanks child | 2.32 | 2.34 | 2.35 | 2.34 | 2.39 |

*Source:* E. Thomson, S. S. McLanahan, and R. B. Curtin, "Family Structure, Gender, and Parental Socialization," *Journal of Marriage and the Family,* 54 (May 1992): 368–378. Results are based on the National Survey of Families and Households.

*Note:* All numbers are adjusted for sex, race, mother's education, father's education, number of siblings, and place of residence. Statistically significant differences from two-parent families are in bold type.

Remarried mothers and mothers living with partners are the least involved with their children. They share fewer meals, they read to their children less often, and they participate in fewer outside activities. Again, while none of these differences is large, they accumulate over time and they are statistically significant. The lower levels of involvement among remarried and cohabiting mothers provide some support for the notion that stepfathers compete with children for the mother's time. Rather than increasing the time available to mothers to spend time with their children, having a stepfather or male partner in the household appears to reduce it.

This is not as bad as it may seem, however. If we add stepfather's time to mother's time, having a stepfather or male partner in the house *increases* the total amount of parental time available to children in stepfamilies as compared with single-parent families. Although stepfathers and cohabiting partners spend less time with the children in the household than resident biological fathers, they spend *more* time than nonresident biological fathers. Thus the total amount of parental time in stepfamilies and mother–partner families is greater on average than the total amount of parental time in single-mother families.

In a small number of families, children in stepfamilies may actually have more parental time than children in two-parent families, as in the case where a child has frequent contact with a mother and stepfather as well as the nonresident father (and perhaps a stepmother). Families that fit this description are rare, however, as can be seen from Figure 12. Nor is it clear that the extra time, when divided among three or four parents rather than two, is as beneficial to the child as the time spent with two parents who live in the same household. Again, if the nonresident parent gets along well with the biological parent and stepparent, the additional time probably has a positive effect on the child. If the adults do not get along, it may actually be harmful.

Quality of time spent with children, as well as quantity, was of interest to us, and so we measured positive interaction between mother and child by asking mothers how often they hugged or praised their child in the past week. We measured negative inter-

## TABLE 7
## Parental supervision (measured by percentage of mothers answering yes).

| Question put to mother | Two-parent family | Mother and stepfather | Mother and partner | Divorced mother | Never-married mother |
|---|---|---|---|---|---|
| Child never left alone? | 31.1% | 28.1% | **20.4%** | **25.5%** | **19.3%** |
| Know child's whereabouts? | 88.3 | 89.1 | 86.8 | 87.3 | 88.8 |
| Child has curfew? | 9.1 | 9.2 | 9.0 | 9.1 | 9.0 |
| Child has bedtime? | 8.8 | 8.7 | 8.8 | **8.7** | 8.7 |
| Child has TV rules? | 35.9 | 32.2 | **19.4** | **31.9** | **29.6** |
| Child has chores? | 50.9 | 55.1 | 48.1 | 51.9 | **44.4** |

*Source:* E. Thomson, S. S. McLanahan, and R. B. Curtin, "Family Structure, Gender, and Parental Socialization," *Journal of Marriage and the Family,* 54 (May 1992): 368–378. Results are based on data from the National Survey of Families and Households, 1987.

*Note:* All numbers are adjusted for sex, race, mother's education, father's education, number of siblings, and place of residence. Statistically significant differences from two-parent families are in bold type.

action by asking how often mothers spanked or scolded the child. While scolding a child is not necessarily an indicator of "bad" parenting—some children need scolding sometimes—it does tell us about the frequency of negative interactions. Too much scolding suggests a breakdown in parental authority. The only piece of evidence we found to suggest that the quality of time spent with children is lower in single-parent families is that never-married mothers report giving fewer hugs and less praise to their children than other mothers (Table 6).

Again, we should point out that researchers who have directly observed mothers and children in single-parent families have painted a less rosy picture of the mother-child relationship, especially in the months immediately following a separation or divorce, and especially when the mother is young and poor.[7] Since the results reported in Table 6 are based on mothers' reports rather than direct observation, they may reflect some degree of denial on the part of mothers. In the next section we will compare mothers' reports to children's reports of parental involvement.

Parental control was measured by a set of questions that asked whether a child is required to inform his parents about where he is going, whether a child is allowed to stay at home alone, whether he has a curfew, and whether there are rules about bedtime, household chores, and TV watching. The numbers in Table 7 represent the percentage of mothers in each category who answered yes to these questions. The information is based on age-appropriate samples: questions about bedtime were only asked of children between the ages of five and eleven, whereas questions about supervision were asked of all children.

Single mothers exercise less control over their children than mothers in two-parent families. Never-married mothers are especially lenient; only 19 percent say they never leave their child alone, as compared with 31 percent of married mothers and 25.5 percent of divorced mothers. The pattern for bedtime, TV watching, and household chores is similar to that for supervision: single mothers report having fewer rules than married mothers. In contrast, remarried mothers report about the same levels of supervision as mothers in two-parent families.

Does the presence of a grandmother or other adult affect the level of adult supervision? In Chapter 2 we argued that supervision might be higher when a grandmother lived in the household and might be lower when the mother was cohabiting. We expected grandmothers to reinforce supervision since they share a commitment to the child. We expected male partners to undermine supervision because they compete with children for the mothers' time. We found that 32 percent of mothers living with a grandmother or other relative reported never leaving a child alone, whereas only 20 percent of mothers living with a male partner gave this answer. If we compare these numbers with those in Table 7 we see that having a grandmother in the house does increase parental supervision, whereas having a male partner does not. Twenty-eight percent of remarried mothers report never leaving their child alone. The fact that mothers who live with a male partner are more lenient with their children than mothers who are remarried suggests that stepfathers are more likely to assume parental responsibilities than male partners in general.

## CHILDREN'S REPORTS OF PARENTAL BEHAVIOR

In addition to information obtained from mothers, we also have data from children about the behavior of their parents. The High School and Beyond Study asks students whether their parents help with schoolwork and whether they supervise their social activities. It also asks about parent–child communication.

According to high school sophomores, divorced parents provide less help with homework and less supervision than married parents (Table 8). The differences in parental investment are somewhat larger when children do the reporting than when parents do the reporting, which is about what we would expect. Mothers are likely to overestimate their involvement, whereas children probably underestimate mothers' involvement. Children of single mothers report talking to their mothers more often than children in two-

### TABLE 8
**Children's reports of high parental involvement and supervision (measured by percentage answering yes).**

| Family type | Mother helps with schoolwork | Father helps with schoolwork | Parental supervision | Talks with parents |
|---|---|---|---|---|
| Two-parent families | 90% | 81% | 84% | 40% |
| Single-parent families | **85** | **56** | **75** | **44** |
| Stepfamilies | **85** | **68** | 82 | **37** |

*Source:* High School and Beyond Study. All statistically significant differences from two-parent families are in bold type.
*Note:* Parental involvement measured at sophomore year.

parent families. This finding is consistent with the argument that single mothers rely on their children as confidants.

Whether being a confidant is good or bad for a child is hard to say. Some researchers emphasize the potentially negative consequences associated with the "loss of childhood" that often comes with growing up with a single parent and assuming adult responsibilities early in adolescence. Others have noted that many of these children grow up to be more independent than their peers, which may increase their chances of success later on.

### PARENTAL ASPIRATIONS

One of the most consistent findings in the literature on educational attainment is that children whose parents have high expectations and high aspirations are more successful than children whose parents are less ambitious, even after taking academic ability and social class background into account.[8]

The HSB study asked students whether or not their parents *expect*

### TABLE 9
### Children's reports of high parental aspirations
### (measured by percentage answering yes).

| Family type | HSB | NLSY |
| --- | --- | --- |
| Two-parent families | 47.5% | 64.7% |
| Single-parent families | **45.3** | **63.6** |
| Stepfamilies | **40.6** | 65.1 |

*Sources:* High School and Beyond Study and National Longitudinal Survey of Youth.

*Note:* All numbers are adjusted for sex, race, mother's education, father's education, number of siblings, and place of residence. Statistically significant differences from two-parent families are in bold type.

them to graduate from college, and the NLSY study asked them whether their parents (or other significant adults) will be *disappointed* if they do not go to college. Children in one-parent households are less likely to answer yes to these questions than children in two-parent families (Table 9). In the HSB study, however, children in stepfamilies are just as likely to report high parental expectations.

Another way that parents influence children is by serving as role models. In Chapter 2 we argued that children from one-parent families were probably more accepting of single parenthood than children from two-parent families, in part because they have been socialized to value single parenthood more (or to view it less negatively) and in part because they have more information about how single parents manage their lives. The HSB survey questions students about their attitudes toward nonmarital childbearing—whether they would consider having a child out of wedlock—and we used this question as an indicator of the role-model effect.

Not surprisingly, sons and daughters in single-parent families and stepfamilies were much more likely to approve of out-of-wedlock childbearing. This was true even after we adjusted for differences in race and parental education. Growing up in a household with only one biological parent clearly makes children more accepting of single motherhood.

## FAMILY DISRUPTION AND CHANGES IN PARENTING

It should be fairly clear by now that parents in one-parent families are somewhat less involved with their children than parents in two-parent families. But what we don't know is whether the differences in parenting predate the parents' decision to separate, or whether it is a consequence of that decision. If, as some people have argued, parental conflict is causing both family disruption and school problems, we would expect to find evidence of less parental involvement before the separation. Indeed, if conflict is high, we might expect parenting to improve after the parents separate.

To determine whether or not family disruption leads to a decline in parental investment, and to determine whether parents who end their marriage are less involved with their children even before they divorce, we limited our sample to high school students who were living with both parents in their sophomore year. We then compared students whose parents broke up between their sophomore and senior years with students whose parents stayed together.

We should point out that using a two-year window to assess changes in parents' behavior can be misleading. First, we are measuring predivorce behavior very close to the time of the separation. This means that our predivorce measure may pick up some of the effect of the impending divorce, in which case it will be biased in a negative direction and will cause us to underestimate the quality of predivorce parenting.

On the other hand, we are measuring postdivorce behavior very soon after the divorce. Hetherington and her colleagues found that the first eighteen months after separation were the most difficult for mothers and children.[9] Thus, to the extent that the postdivorce measure of parenting is capturing the effects of a recent divorce, it will underestimate the quality of postdivorce parenting.

---

### TABLE 10
### Change in parental involvement, supervision, and aspirations between the sophomore and senior years.

| Family type | Mother's involvement | Father's involvement | Parental supervision | Talks with child | Parental aspirations |
|---|---|---|---|---|---|
| Stable families | −1 | −1 | −2 | −10 | 4 |
| Unstable families | **−10** | **−19** | **−13** | **−20** | −2 |

*Source:* High School and Beyond Study.

*Note:* Stable families are defined as those in which the parents did not separate or divorce between the sophomore and senior years; unstable families are defined as those in which the parents separated or divorced. Statistically significant differences from two-parent families are in bold.

---

Parental involvement and supervision decline for all children between the sophomore and senior years, but the decline is greater for children whose parents separate than for children whose families remain intact (see Table 10). Moreover, whereas parental aspirations increase slightly during those two years for children in two-parent families, they decline for children in disrupted families. These results make it reasonably clear that differences in parental resources between children in two-parent and one-parent families are not due simply to predisruption differences. Rather, disruption is associated with a *decline* in parental resources, at least in the short term.

While the decline in parenting may last only one or two years, the fact that children are in high school when the decline occurs means that it may have lasting consequences for future success. The last two years in high school are a critical time in a child's life, and the loss or lack of parental involvement and aspirations during this time can lead to irrevocable events such as becoming a teen mother or dropping out of high school. Hence, even though the "divorce effect" may last for only one or two years, from the child's point of view it may last a lifetime.

## DOES PARENTING EXPLAIN DIFFERENCES IN
## CHILD WELL-BEING?

We now turn to the most important question, which is whether or not differences in parental practices account for differences in child outcomes. This set of analyses parallels those presented in Chapter 5, only here we look at parenting rather than income and we rely primarily on the HSB survey, supplemented wherever possible with evidence from other surveys.

Figure 13 reports the difference in achievement between children from two-parent and one-parent families before and after parental practices (involvement, supervision, and aspirations) are taken into account. The first bar in each pair shows the difference before adjusting for parental behavior, and the second bar shows the difference in well-being after adjusting for these factors. By comparing the two bars, we can see how much of the difference in child well-being in single-parent families and stepfamilies is accounted for by differences in parenting.[10]

Parenting practices account for over half of the difference in high school dropout between children in single-parent families and children in two-parent families, and it accounts for about 20 percent of the difference between children in stepfamilies and those in two-parent families. (The latter is not statistically significant.) The disparity in high school dropout rates (that is, the difference between children in two-parent families and those in one-parent families) falls from 6 percentage points (baseline) to 3 percentage points when parental involvement is taken into account. In stepfamilies, it falls from 5 to 4. The latter decline is not statistically significant.

The results for early childbearing are very similar to those for high school dropout. Differences in parenting practices explain about 20 percent of the disadvantage associated with single motherhood and none of the disadvantage associated with stepfamilies.

Parenting also accounts for all of the difference in idleness between boys in single-parent and two-parent families. The disparity in the risk of being idle falls to zero when we adjust for differences

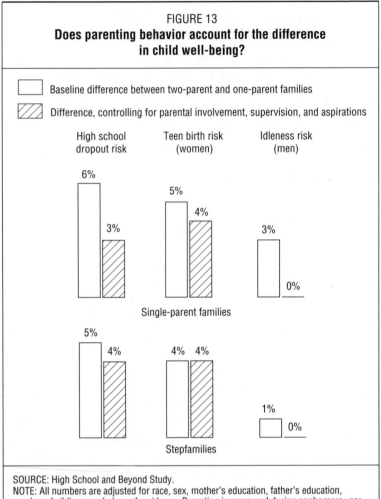

FIGURE 13

**Does parenting behavior account for the difference in child well-being?**

SOURCE: High School and Beyond Study.
NOTE: All numbers are adjusted for race, sex, mother's education, father's education, number of siblings, and place of residence. Parenting is measured during sophomore year.

in parenting. The difference in idleness between boys in stepfamilies and those in two-parent families is virtually zero to begin with.

Other researchers have found weaker parenting effects than we report here. In an earlier study based on the High School and Beyond data, Nan Astone and Sara McLanahan found that parenting practices accounted for only about 10 percent of the difference in dropout rates between children in one-parent and two-parent families, and Thomson, Hanson, and McLanahan reported similar results, using the NSFH parent sample. Furthermore, our own analyses based on the NLSY data (not reported here) showed that differences in parents' college aspirations did not explain any of the differences in child outcomes. Because of these inconsistencies, we are less confident of the parenting results reported in this chapter than the income results reported in Chapter 5, even though they are equally dramatic.[11]

In Chapter 6 we saw that income accounted for about half of the difference in high school dropout rates, teen birth rates, and idleness rates between children in single-parent families as compared with children in two-parent families. We now find that parental aspirations as well as parental involvement and supervision play a large role in explaining the remaining differences in child well-being. The three factors together account for 40 percent of the difference between children in single-parent and two-parent families and possibly for as much as 20 percent of the difference between children in stepfamilies and two-parent families, although the latter decline is not statistically significant.

But would it be accurate to say that we have now accounted for 90 percent of the difference between single-parent families and two-parent families? Not necessarily. It is possible that the two effects—income and parenting—are not independent but are picking up some of the same differences in family resources. Ideally we would like to estimate the effects of income and parenting together in the same model. Since neither the PSID nor the HSB survey has information on both parenting and income, we cannot use either of these two data sets to examine the combined effect. The

NSFH, however, does contain data on both types of resources, and thus we used these data to try to answer our question.

We found that income was not associated with any of the parenting measures we examined, including mothers' and fathers' activities with children, their supervision and rules, and parental goals. The one exception was that mothers with higher income reported leaving their children alone more often than mothers with lower income, but this was due to the fact that mothers in high-income families were more likely to be working outside the home than mothers in low-income families. Once we adjusted for mothers' employment status, income was not related to parenting practices.

We should point out that other researchers using different data sets have found that income *is* related to good parenting.[12] Since the information on parenting in the NSFH is provided by the parents rather than by direct observation from the interviewers, it is possible that our measures of parenting are not as reliable as those used in some of the other studies. It is also possible that the relationships found in the other studies are biased in some other way.

## DO CHANGES IN PARENTING EXPLAIN CHILD OUTCOMES?

To carry the analysis one step further, we examine the effect of changes in parental resources on changes in children's well-being. This approach is preferable to simply looking at the relationship between family structure and parenting at one point in time. It provides a more conservative estimate of the effect of family structure on child well-being, since it allows us to adjust for predivorce differences in parenting.

In order to make this work, we again restricted our sample to students who were living with both parents in their sophomore year, and we compared students whose parents divorced or separated between the sophomore and senior years with students whose parents were married in both years. Since the High School and Beyond Study did not ask students who were not in school their senior year the questions about parental involvement and supervision, we were forced to carry out our analysis on a sample of children who were *in school* both years. This meant that we could not use high school dropout as one of our indicators of success, since practically all the children in our sample finished high school. (Nearly all of the students who were in school their senior year received a diploma or GED.) However, we were able to use early childbearing and idleness as indicators of children's success, since these events occurred even to children who managed to graduate from high school.

By focusing on students who were in school both years, we ignore the children with the most serious problems, including those most severely affected by their parents' separation. We would expect the effect of divorce on changes in parenting and child well-being to be smaller for this group than for all children, and therefore the estimates reported in Figure 14 should be viewed as conservative estimates of the "true" effect of family disruption on parenting and child well-being.

Girls whose parents divorced during high school were 4 percentage points more likely to become teen mothers than girls whose parents remained together. Similarly, boys whose families broke up were 6 percentage points more likely to be idle at age twenty than boys who did not experience a divorce. Notice that the risk of teen birth associated with a disruption in high school is only 1 percentage point smaller than the risk associated with living with a single parent at age sixteen, whereas the risk of idleness is even higher (Figure 13). The latter is surprising since we would have expected children with the most serious problems to have dropped out of school by their senior year and therefore be missing from our sample. The fact that we find effects of this magnitude even when we exclude high school dropouts suggests that family disruption during the high school years can be quite devastating to young men.

The difference in the risk of teen childbearing—4 percentage points—does not change very much when we adjust for predivorce parenting practices. It goes down half a percentage point, but the

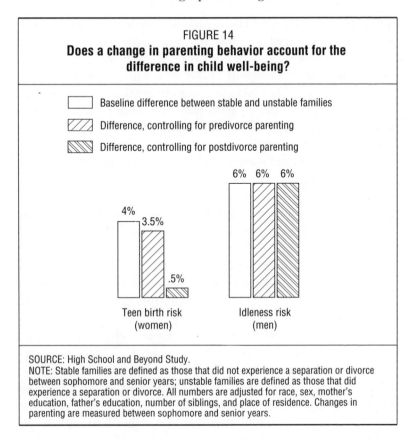

FIGURE 14
**Does a change in parenting behavior account for the difference in child well-being?**

☐ Baseline difference between stable and unstable families

▨ Difference, controlling for predivorce parenting

▧ Difference, controlling for postdivorce parenting

Teen birth risk
(women)

Idleness risk
(men)

SOURCE: High School and Beyond Study.
NOTE: Stable families are defined as those that did not experience a separation or divorce between sophomore and senior years; unstable families are defined as those that did experience a separation or divorce. All numbers are adjusted for race, sex, mother's education, father's education, number of siblings, and place of residence. Changes in parenting are measured between sophomore and senior years.

decline is not statistically significant. The difference goes away entirely when we adjust for postdivorce parental involvement, however. In other words, the decline in parental involvement and supervision can account for *all* of the increased risk of early childbearing among young women who experience a parental divorce during high school.

The results for idleness among young men follow a different pattern. The difference in the risk of idleness among young men whose parents divorce and those whose parents stay together—6 percentage points—does not change when we adjust for differences in parenting practices before or after divorce. Since we are looking at a subset of boys from disrupted families—those who did not drop out of school—we cannot conclude that changes in parenting are unrelated to increases in the risk of idleness for young men whose parents divorce during high school. Young men who experienced the greatest declines in parenting and who subsequently had trouble finding and keeping a job may have dropped out of school by their senior year and therefore be missing from our sample. We can say, however, that for young men who remain in school, changes in parental involvement and supervision are not responsible for their increased risk of idleness later on.

The evidence that changes in parental resources accompanying divorce increase the risk of early childbearing reinforces our belief that negative outcomes among children whose parents end their marriage are not simply caused by characteristics that predate divorce. While we cannot be sure that an unknown variable is not causing both the change in parenting and the change in marital status, the estimates presented in Figure 14 are a more conservative test of the argument that family disruption itself leads to lower child well-being.

We have now seen that changes in both economic resources and parental resources account for a good deal of the difference between children in two-parent families and those in single-parent families, and for some of the difference in stepfamilies. In the next chapter we will examine the role of community resources in determining children's success, and in particular we will try to discover whether these changes have a special effect on stepfamilies.

# CHAPTER SEVEN

# THE COMMUNITY CONNECTION

Besides needing parents who are willing (and able) to share their time and money, young people also need resources outside the family to help them grow into independent, successful adults. They need good teachers to stimulate their minds and help them develop their intellectual capacities, they need good neighbors to reinforce their parents and provide additional support and supervision, and they need communities that are willing to invest their tax dollars in institutions that serve children—schools, recreational programs, safe neighborhoods.[1] In this chapter, we examine the relationship between family disruption and children's community resources, and we ask whether differences in resources can account for why children in single-parent families and stepfamilies are more likely to drop out of high school, become teen mothers, and become idle than children in two-parent families.

We focus on two aspects of community resources: the *level of resources* in a child's community, and the *connections* between the child and members of the community. Knowing whether a community has good schools and other resources for children is not sufficient for knowing whether a child benefits from these resources. In order to take full advantage of whatever a community offers, a child must know and trust his neighbors and teachers, and they must know and care about him. This is what social capital is about.

## THE LEVEL OF COMMUNITY RESOURCES

We begin by asking whether a family's structure is related to the quality of the community in which the family resides. The PSID contains information on the characteristics of the census tracts in which families reside, and we use this information to compare the physical environments of children in two-parent and one-parent families.[2] We focus on seven indicators of community quality: percent of families living below the poverty line, percent of families headed by single women,[3] percent of families receiving Aid to Families with Dependent Children (AFDC), percent of men over age sixteen unemployed, percent of housing units vacant, percent of young adults without a high school diploma, and whether or not the census tract is an "underclass area." The latter is defined as a tract in which high school dropout rates, welfare payment receipts, poverty rates, and unemployment rates are all at least one standard deviation above the mean for the nation as a whole.[4] The underclass indicator incorporates many of the other measures of community quality, but it is a much more extreme measure of community deprivation. In order to be classified as "underclass," a community, or census tract, must score very high on several indicators.

Differences in census tract characteristics for single-parent and two-parent families are reported in Table 11. (Two-parent families include stepfamilies in this table.) We examine whites and blacks separately, since we know from other studies that residential segregation by race is very high and that blacks are much more likely to live in disadvantaged areas than whites.[5] Our findings confirm these results. White children are much more likely to live in well-off communities than black children, regardless of family structure. White children in single-parent families are much better off than black children in two-parent families in terms of these measures of community quality.

But family structure, while not as important as race in predicting the quality of the communities in which children live, is also highly correlated with the quality of community resources available to

## TABLE 11
### Characteristics of census tracts where children live, by race and by family structure.

| Race and family type | Poverty rate of census tract | Percent of female-headed families in census tract | AFDC rate of census tract | Jobless father rate of census tract | Percent of vacant buildings in census tract | High school dropout rate of census tract |
|---|---|---|---|---|---|---|
| **Whites** | | | | | | |
| Two-parent families | 8.7% | 12.2% | 5.9% | 30.0% | 5.0% | 9.9% |
| One-parent families | 11.0 | 16.3 | 7.5 | 30.4 | 6.6 | 12.5 |
| **Blacks** | | | | | | |
| Two-parent families | 23.8 | 30.1 | 16.8 | 39.9 | 8.3 | 17.4 |
| One-parent families | 26.0 | 36.5 | 20.6 | 41.8 | 9.0 | 19.5 |

*Source:* Panel Study of Income Dynamics, census tract data, characteristics file.
*Note:* In this table, stepfamilies are combined with two–parent families.

children and their parents. White children in single-parent families live in neighborhoods with substantially higher rates of poverty, female headship, welfare use, and high school failure than white children in two-parent families. Differences in joblessness and vacant housing are not significant.

Among black children, the contrast in community quality by family structure is much smaller than among whites, but high enough to put 4 percent of black children from single-parent families into "underclass" areas (not shown in table). Since a census tract must be at least one standard deviation above the national mean on rates of high school dropout, welfare participation, poverty, and unemployment to be labeled underclass, neighborhoods that qualify are very rare. According to these data, less than 0.5 percent of all white children, and less than 1 percent of black children in two-parent families, were living in underclass areas in 1980. The small percentage of people who were living in such areas, however, were exposed to conditions of extreme hardship and deprivation.[6]

The fact that so few families live in underclass areas and the fact that single-parent black families are disproportionately represented there are consistent with William Julius Wilson's argument that during the 1960s and 1970s working-class and middle-class black families were able to move out of the worst neighborhoods in urban central cities, leaving behind the most disadvantaged families.[7] Unfortunately, single mothers, who are probably the least able to cope with underclass conditions, are the most likely to remain in these areas. Massey and Denton have shown that increases in poverty rates also contributed to the growing concentration of poor people in underclass neighborhoods during the 1970s and 1980s.[8]

## SCHOOL QUALITY

Perhaps the best way to assess children's access to community resources is to examine their schools. Compared with children from two-parent families, children from one-parent families are more likely to attend schools with high dropout rates (Figure 15).[9] School quality by this measure is lower for children in both single-parent

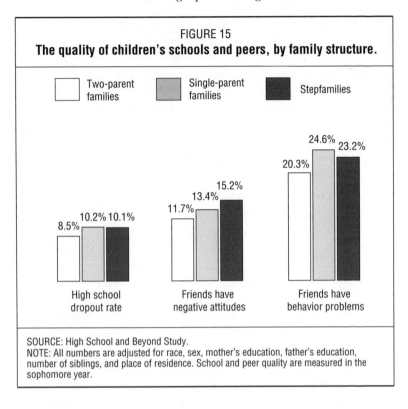

FIGURE 15
**The quality of children's schools and peers, by family structure.**

☐ Two-parent families ▨ Single-parent families ■ Stepfamilies

High school dropout rate: 8.5%, 10.2%, 10.1%

Friends have negative attitudes: 11.7%, 13.4%, 15.2%

Friends have behavior problems: 20.3%, 24.6%, 23.2%

SOURCE: High School and Beyond Study.
NOTE: All numbers are adjusted for race, sex, mother's education, father's education, number of siblings, and place of residence. School and peer quality are measured in the sophomore year.

families and stepfamilies, as compared with children in two-parent families. According to the NLSY, school quality is lower (dropout rates are higher) only for children in single-parent families.

Children from one-parent families, and especially children who do not have a stepparent, attend schools with a higher percentage of minority students and minority teachers than children in two-parent families. The average child from a single-parent family attends a school that is 22 percent black while the average child in a two-parent family attends a school that is 12 percent black. Because our numbers are adjusted for differences in race and other family background factors, we know that they do not simply reflect the fact that children in one-parent families are more likely to be black and Hispanic themselves.

While going to a school that is racially diverse can enhance a child's educational experiences and while some middle-class parents seek out such schools for their children, on average schools with more minority students spend less money per child, and have higher teacher/student ratios, than schools with fewer minorities. This is because public school financing is community-based and schools with a high concentration of minority students usually have a low tax base. The fact that children from one-parent families are also more likely to report that their school facilities are in poor condition supports the notion that these children are attending less well-funded schools.

Do adolescents in one-parent families choose friends who are less motivated toward schoolwork than adolescents in two-parent families? Do they hang out with children who cause problems for teachers and school administrators? Based on information collected from students during their sophomore year, the answer to both these questions is yes (Figure 15). Compared with children from two-parent families, children from single-parent families and step-families are more likely to report that their friends create problems for teachers and school administrators and do not value education. The differences in peer quality are not large, but they are statistically significant.

When we look at whether family instability leads to *changes* in peer quality between the sophomore and senior years, we get a somewhat different picture. Students whose parents separated in high school reported a decline in the attitudes of friends toward school, but no increase in antisocial behavior. We believe the latter is due to that fact that many of the students in the HSB Study did not answer the questions about peer quality in their senior year, especially children from one-parent families. Some of this missing data was attributable to the fact that students had dropped out of school, and some of it to the fact that students were absent and not interviewed. We suspect that if the information had been more complete, we would have observed a steeper decline in peer quality as measured by antisocial behavior among children whose parents broke up. However, we have no direct evidence to support this suspicion.

## RESIDENTIAL MOBILITY VERSUS STABILITY

The information about census tracts, county-level characteristics, schools, and peer quality tells us that children in one-parent families live in communities with fewer resources than do children in two-parent families. This information is useful in giving us a sense of children's exposure to hardship conditions. But the ties between children and community resources may be even more important for their well-being than the level of resources per se. Two children living in the same community may have very different relationships with their neighbors and very different information about school personnel, afterschool programs, enrichment courses, organized sports activities, libraries, museums, and so on, and thus their social capital in the community may be much lower than that of other children living in the same neighborhood.

Residential stability is a reasonably good indicator of social capital because it measures the potential for long-standing connections between the child's family and other adults in the community. Even in very poor communities, people with social capital are better off than people without social capital. Carol Stack's book *All Our Kin* shows how individuals with limited financial resources can improve their lives by pooling resources and participating in exchange networks with friends and neighbors.

A residential move is not necessarily a bad thing for a family as a whole. Families often move because a parent is offered a better job in another city or because the family can afford a house in a more desirable location. Sometimes a family moves so that the child can attend a better school. Even under favorable conditions such as these, however, moving can be a very painful experience for a child. Being the new kid on the block or in school is scary, and some children react by withdrawing or "acting out" in ways that undermine their school performance. Others fall in with the "wrong crowd" because they feel like outsiders. Making new friends and adjusting to a new neighborhood can be especially stressful for children who are simultaneously adjusting to the loss of a parent, or the arrival of a stepparent.

---

## TABLE 12
### Residential mobility, measured by family moves per year.

| Family type | HSB | PSID |
|---|---|---|
| Two-parent families | 1.45 | 1.36 |
| Single-parent families | **1.84** | **2.65** |
| Stepfamilies | **2.11** | **3.40** |

*Source:* High School and Beyond Study and Panel Study of Income Dynamics.

*Note:* All numbers are adjusted for race, sex, mother's education, father's education, number of siblings, and place of residence. All differences from two-parent families are statistically significant.

---

Three of our data sets provide information on residential mobility. The HSB asks respondents about the number of times they moved since the fifth grade, the PSID provides information on the number of moves since age eight, and the NLSY provides information on whether or not a family moved at least once during high school. The relationship between family structure and residential mobility based on the HSB and PSID surveys is shown in Table 12. (These numbers are adjusted for differences in background characteristics.)

Children who live with both parents experience the least residential mobility of all children, whereas children who live in a stepfamily experience the most mobility. The average child from a two-parent family experienced approximately 1.5 moves, according to our two surveys, while the average child from a stepfamily experienced between 2 and 3.5 moves. Overall, the level of mobility is somewhat higher in the PSID data than in the HSB study, but this is to be expected, given the way in which mobility is defined in these two surveys. In order to count as a move, a student in the HSB data had to change school, whereas in the PSID all moves were counted, regardless of the circumstances.

## TABLE 13
## Residential mobility, by type of move.

| Family type | Total moves | Reason for move | | | |
| --- | --- | --- | --- | --- | --- |
| | | Productive | Consumption | Involuntary | Other |
| Two–parent families | 100% | 21% | 49% | 15% | 15% |
| Single–parent families | 100 | 6 | 46 | 34 | 15 |
| Stepfamilies | 100 | 14 | 39 | 14 | 32 |

*Source:* Panel Study of Income Dynamics.
*Note:* "Other" includes moves during the year of family disruption for remarriage.

The NLSY measure of mobility is somewhat different from the measures in the other surveys; it is a dichotomous variable that simply tells us whether or not the child's family moved between 1979 and 1983. The NLSY data tell us that about 22 percent of children from two-parent families, about 28 percent of children from single-parent families, and 43 percent of children from step-families experienced a move during early adolescence.[10]

The PSID asks parents why they moved, and we used these data as a way of assessing the potential effect of the move on children's well-being (Table 13). Was the primary motivation to get a better job (a productive move) or to bring housing expenses in line with income (a consumption move)? Or did the family move because of an eviction or some other involuntary reason? The answers to these questions tell us something about the conditions under which a move occurred. Presumably a move for either productive or consumption reasons is preferable to a move for involuntary reasons.

We found that most families moved in order to get a better house or to get housing that was better suited to their immediate needs. Forty-nine percent of the moves among two-parent families were of this sort, as were 46 percent of the moves among single-parent families. Thirty-nine percent of moves among stepfamilies were for consumption reasons, whereas 32 percent were for "other" reasons. We classified all moves that occurred in the same year as a divorce or remarriage as "other."

After consumption, the next most important reason for moving for two-parent families was to get a better job or improve employment opportunities. Twenty-one percent of two-parent families that moved gave this as their reason for moving, as compared with 6 percent of single-parent families and 14 percent of stepfamilies. As for involuntary moves, 34 percent of single-parent families that moved did so unwillingly, because they were evicted or could no longer afford the rent. Less than half that rate was reported among two-parent families and stepfamilies.

Altogether, these numbers indicate that children in single-parent families experience the most stressful moves, whereas children in stepfamilies experience the most moves. We believe that both situations contribute to the breakdown of community ties.

## DO COMMUNITY RESOURCES EXPLAIN DIFFERENCES IN CHILD WELL-BEING?

In the previous discussion we showed that children in disrupted families (as compared with two-parent families) live in communities with fewer resources, they move more often (and more often for involuntary reasons), and as a result they have weaker connections to community resources. We now ask whether these differences account for the difference in child well-being in one-parent and two-parent families.

The baseline differential for high school graduation is 6 percentage points for children in single-parent families and 5 percentage points for children in stepfamilies, as compared with children in two-parent families, according to HSB data (Figure 16). After taking school quality into account (second bar), the single-parent difference remains at 6 points (indicating that school quality is not a factor in explaining the higher risk of dropping out of school), while the stepfamily difference falls from 5 to 4 percentage points.

(The decline in the stepfamily differential is not statistically significant.)

After taking both school quality and residential mobility into account (third bar), the single-parent effect falls to 5 percentage points, and the stepfamily effect falls to 3 points. The drop in the stepfamily differential is statistically significant and shows that community factors account for about 40 percent of the difference in high school graduation between children in two-parent families and children in stepfamilies. This is the first time we have identified a mechanism capable of explaining the disadvantage associated with stepfamilies. In the previous two chapters, we found that economic and parenting resources accounted for a good deal of the difference between children in single-parent families and two-parent families but not much of the difference between children in stepfamilies and two-parent families. Now we find that school quality, and especially residential mobility, account for as much as 40 percent of the disadvantage associated with living in a stepfamily.

With a colleague, Nan Astone, we looked at the effects of residential mobility on children's school attendance and whether they *ever* drop out of school (including children who eventually graduated), as well as the effect on high school graduation. We found a similar pattern for each of these outcomes. Residential mobility accounted for between 35 and 40 percent of the difference in attendance and ever dropping out between children in stepfamilies and two-parent families and it accounted for about 10 percent of the difference in these two outcomes between children in single-parent and two-parent families.[11]

The HSB data contain information on both parenting and community resources, and the fourth bar in Figure 16 reports the difference in graduation rates after taking community resources (as measured by school quality and residential mobility) *and* parental resources into account. By adding parenting resources to our model, we can see if the latter account for any additional part of the family disruption effect, above and beyond that associated with community resources. If parenting behavior and community resources were uncorrelated, the single-parent dropout differential should fall an-

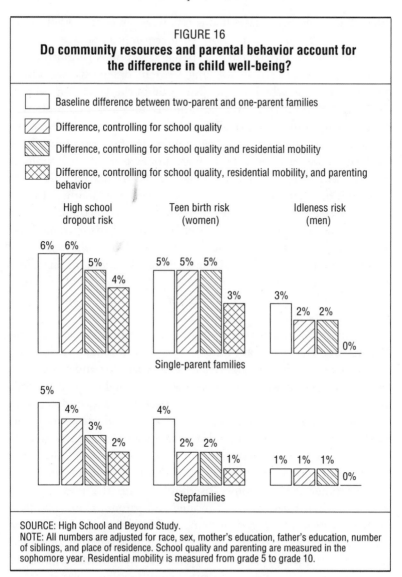

FIGURE 16

**Do community resources and parental behavior account for the difference in child well-being?**

☐ Baseline difference between two-parent and one-parent families

▨ Difference, controlling for school quality

▨ Difference, controlling for school quality and residential mobility

▨ Difference, controlling for school quality, residential mobility, and parenting behavior

SOURCE: High School and Beyond Study.
NOTE: All numbers are adjusted for race, sex, mother's education, father's education, number of siblings, and place of residence. School quality and parenting are measured in the sophomore year. Residential mobility is measured from grade 5 to grade 10.

other 3 percentage points when parental resources are added to the model. (Recall that in the previous chapter, parental resources reduced the single-parent differential by 3 percentage points.) Adjusting for parental resources reduces the single-parent differential by only 1 percentage point, which means that some of the parenting effect is associated with differences in community resources and mobility.

When we look at stepfamilies, we find that adding parental resources to the model reduces the stepfamily effect on high school graduation by one more percentage point, from 3 to 2. This is exactly what we would have expected if parental resources and community resources were independent of one another. In the previous chapter, taking parental resources into account reduced the baseline difference between stepfamilies and two-parent families by 1 percentage point (see Figure 13). When we adjust for parental resources, the second bar in Figure 16 drops by one additional percentage point.

The pattern is slightly different for teen births. Differences in school quality account for about half of the stepfamily effect and for none of the single-parent effect. Differences in residential mobility, however, do not account for *any* of the difference in early childbearing for either children in single-parent families or stepfamilies. Finally, including the controls for parental behavior further reduces the differential for both single-parent families and stepfamilies, indicating that parenting has an additional effect on child well-being in regard to early childbearing, even after taking community resources into account.

The numbers for idleness are also different from the numbers for the other two outcomes, as they were in the previous two chapters when we considered money and parenting. For this particular measure of child well-being, community resources appear to account for more of the single-parent family differential and for less of the stepfamily differential. Children in stepfamilies are not very different from children in two-parent families when it comes to being idle, at least in these data, and therefore we do not give much weight to the fact that community resources do not "account for" any of the stepfamily effect.

The role of community resources is not as pronounced when

we examine the NLSY results (not reported in a figure). These data have only one measure of community quality (school dropout rate), and the measure of residential mobility is limited to whether or not a move occurred during high school. Nevertheless, the pattern in these data is quite similar to the pattern observed in the HSB. School quality and mobility account for about 10 percent of the disadvantage associated with living in a single-parent family and for 25 percent of the disadvantage associated with living in a stepfamily. Again, community factors matter more for children in stepfamilies than for children in single-parent families.

The PSID estimates are different from the estimates based on the other data sets. The PSID has information on both residential mobility and income, and therefore we can use these data to determine whether the two types of resources have independent effects on children. If residential mobility is just another indicator of family income, the policy implications would be different than if it has an independent effect.

According to Figure 17, two thirds of the difference between children in single-parent families and two-parent families is due to differences in residential mobility. The rest is due to family income. Income and residential mobility together account for all of the educational disadvantage of children living in single-parent families!

Residential mobility is even more important in accounting for differences between children in stepfamilies and children in two-parent families. As shown in Figure 17, it accounts for almost all of the disadvantage in high school graduation rates associated with living in a stepfamily.

The pattern for teen birth is similar to the pattern for dropping out of high school. Residential mobility accounts for just less than half of the difference between children in two-parent and single-parent families, and it accounts for over half of the difference between children in stepfamilies and two-parent families. If we also adjust for income in the case of single parents, the two factors together almost eliminate the effect of single parenthood on early childbearing, as they did in the case of high school graduation. Again, income is not a factor in explaining the stepfamily differential.

Residential mobility is less important in accounting for differ-

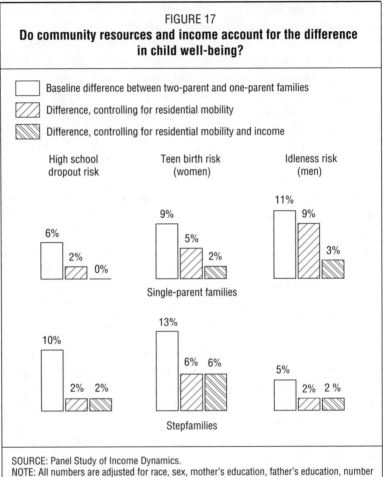

FIGURE 17

**Do community resources and income account for the difference in child well-being?**

☐ Baseline difference between two-parent and one-parent families

▨ Difference, controlling for residential mobility

▨ Difference, controlling for residential mobility and income

High school dropout risk | Teen birth risk (women) | Idleness risk (men)

Single-parent families

Stepfamilies

SOURCE: Panel Study of Income Dynamics.
NOTE: All numbers are adjusted for race, sex, mother's education, father's education, number of siblings, and place of residence. Residential mobility is measured between ages 8 and 16. Family income is measured at age 16.

ences in idleness between children in two-parent and single-parent families, although again the overall pattern is the same as it was for the other indicators of child well-being. Mobility accounts for about 60 percent of the difference between children in stepfamilies and children in two-parent families.

### DOES POSTDIVORCE MOBILITY EXPLAIN CHILD OUTCOMES?

As in previous chapters, we must determine whether community quality and residential mobility effects are really due to parents' divorce or whether families that break up are just more likely to live in poorer neighborhoods and move more often. By confining our analysis to a sample of children that we can observe before and after divorce and by looking at residential moves that occur after a divorce we can obtain a better picture of the effect of divorce on *changes* in community resources and changes in child well-being.

In Figure 18 we use a sample of children from the PSID who were living with both parents at age twelve, and we distinguish between those whose parents stayed together and those whose parents broke up between ages twelve and seventeen. This is the same sample used in Chapter 6 to determine the effect of changes in economic resources on child well-being. What we want to do is examine the effect of two adjustments—residential mobility and income—on high school graduation, nonmarital teen births, and idleness at two points in time, in order to determine if a change in those factors can account for a decline in child well-being.

Residential mobility and changes in income have independent effects on all three outcomes. Residential mobility accounts for 25 percent of the increase in the risk of dropping out of high school, and family income and residential mobility combined account for about 60 percent of the difference in risk. Similarly, residential mobility accounts for nearly 30 percent of the increase in the risk of a teen birth, and the two factors combined account for nearly 60 percent of the difference. In contrast, postdivorce mobility has no effect on idleness among young men, whereas declines in in-

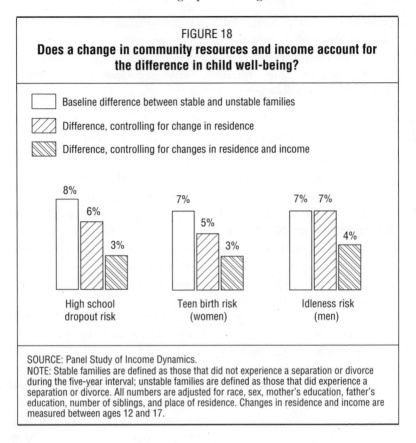

FIGURE 18

**Does a change in community resources and income account for the difference in child well-being?**

☐ Baseline difference between stable and unstable families

▨ Difference, controlling for change in residence

▨ Difference, controlling for changes in residence and income

High school dropout risk: 8%, 6%, 3%

Teen birth risk (women): 7%, 5%, 3%

Idleness risk (men): 7%, 7%, 4%

SOURCE: Panel Study of Income Dynamics.
NOTE: Stable families are defined as those that did not experience a separation or divorce during the five-year interval; unstable families are defined as those that did experience a separation or divorce. All numbers are adjusted for race, sex, mother's education, father's education, number of siblings, and place of residence. Changes in residence and income are measured between ages 12 and 17.

come account for over 40 percent of the difference between young men whose parents stay together and young men whose parents separate.

## SUMMARY

Children raised in one-parent families are disadvantaged in a number of different ways in terms of access to community resources. They are more likely to live in disadvantaged neighborhoods, more likely to associate with peers who have negative attitudes toward school, and more likely to change residences.

These differences in school quality and residential mobility imply that children in one-parent families, and especially children in stepfamilies, have weaker connections to their friends and neighbors and therefore less social capital than children in two-parent families. And indeed, adjusting for differences in school quality and residential mobility eliminates a large part of the difference in the risk of dropping out of high school between children in two-parent families and stepfamilies.

We have now identified a potential mechanism for explaining some of the disadvantages associated with living in a stepfamily. Previously, researchers have only been able to account for differences between children in single-parent and two-parent families. These results are important because residential mobility is something many parents have a good deal of control over. It is always nice to identify a mechanism that can be manipulated, as opposed to something like parents' race or age at birth that cannot be changed. Since many parents are in a position to reduce the number of times they move, and since judges are often in a position to limit or minimize residential mobility, these findings may be especially useful to parents and policymakers in improving the lives of children.

# CHAPTER EIGHT

# WHAT SHOULD BE DONE

Profound changes have occurred in children's family life—changes that will affect over half the next generation. Whereas thirty years ago the typical child was born to married parents and lived with both parents throughout childhood and adolescence, the average child today is expected to live apart from at least one parent before reaching adulthood, and a substantial minority of children are expected never to live with both biological parents. Throughout this book we have focused on what these changes mean for children. We have demonstrated that children raised apart from one of their parents are less successful in adulthood than children raised by both parents, and that many of their problems result from a loss of income, parental involvement and supervision, and ties to the community. For children living with a single parent and no stepparent, income is the single most important factor in accounting for their lower well-being as compared with children living with both parents. It accounts for as much as half of their disadvantage. Low parental involvement, supervision, and aspirations and greater residential mobility account for the rest. The last factor—residential mobility—also accounts for as much as half of the lower well-being of children in stepfamilies, for whom income is much less of an issue. Before discussing what can and should be done for these children, however, let us look at how family structure affects the rest of society—mothers, fathers, and children living in intact families.

## HOW FAMILY STRUCTURE AFFECTS PARENTS

Numerous studies, including our own, have shown that single mothers are much more likely to be poor and economically insecure than married mothers. They also experience more psychological problems, including depression and anxiety.[1] While some of these problems are due to factors that have nothing to do with family structure, others are due to single parenthood itself. Single mothers not only lose economies of scale when they live alone, they also forgo the economic and emotional support that a second parent can provide. In effect, they must fill two parental roles—primary breadwinner and primary caretaker. Since both jobs are difficult and time-consuming, it should come as no surprise that, compared with married mothers, single mothers experience much more stress.[2]

Being a single mother also limits a woman's ability to pursue a career. Without a partner with whom to share childrearing responsibilities, single mothers have difficulty balancing the demands of work and family. And more often than not, they are faced with the dilemma of having to choose between doing a good job at work and doing a good job at home. While married mothers face this same dilemma, as a group they have more time and money at their disposal than single mothers and are in a better position to deal more flexibly with conflicting demands.

Ironically, while growing economic independence has made it easier for women to become single mothers, the rise in single motherhood may ultimately undermine women's economic equality. It is difficult to see how American women can successfully compete with men in the workplace, unless men assume a greater share of responsibility for children. And yet recent trends suggest that just the opposite is occurring.[3] Women are entering the labor force in greater numbers and increasing their parental obligations by becoming single mothers, while more men are maintaining their same work schedules and assuming less responsibility for children.

Fathers are also negatively affected by family breakup. Although the economic costs of divorce are not as great for men as they are for women, fathers lose economies of scale when they establish a second household, and their standard of living usually declines relative to married fathers.[4] Moreover, there is evidence that marriage improves men's productivity on the job and, as a result, their wages, which implies that divorce reduces men's lifetime earnings, at least for those men who do not quickly remarry.[5] The psychological well-being of fathers is also negatively affected by divorce. Compared with married fathers, divorced fathers experience higher levels of depression and psychological distress.[6] Indeed, the emotional costs of divorce appear to be higher for men than for women. The fact that divorced fathers report higher levels of depression and psychological problems than divorced mothers underscores the fact that a substantial number of fathers suffer terribly from the disruption of their relationship with their children.

Fathers also experience a loss of social ties after a divorce. While residential mobility is high among single mothers and children, it is even higher among fathers who do not live with their children. Moreover, when friends and neighbors are forced to take sides in a contested divorce, it is usually the father who loses out. Fathers who lose contact with their children also lose access to the social capital that children provide access to, in the form of friendships with other parents and, later on, in the form of adult support for aging parents. Divorced fathers receive less help in old age from their children than do married fathers.[7]

## HOW FAMILY STRUCTURE AFFECTS
## ALL FAMILIES

Over the past twenty years, public investments in children have declined relative to public investments in the elderly.[8] This has come about in large part because the elderly are a well-organized interest group that successfully lobbies Congress on its own behalf, whereas children have no political power and no voice. The rapid increase in divorce and nonmarital births in recent years can only widen this gap in the distribution of political resources across generations, for the following reasons.

First, weakened ties between fathers and their children reduce the number of adults in society who are committed to children's issues and who are willing to invest in programs for children. Second, because single parents earn a lower income than two-parent families and pay fewer taxes, less money is available to the school system and other social services in those communities with a high percentage of single parents. This lower tax base reduces the community resources available to all children in that community, including those who live with two parents. Third, single parents also have less spare time than married couples and are therefore less likely to participate in voluntary organizations such as parent-teacher associations, recreational groups, and political organizations.[9]

Finally, single parents are less able to protect their property and their children from predators. Homicide rates and robbery rates, especially among juveniles, are more common in communities with a high proportion of single-mother families, even after adjusting for factors such as income, race, age, density, and city size. Two-parent families keep crime rates low not by physically stopping criminal acts but by controlling activities among youths that set the stage for crime, such as vandalism, hanging out, and so on.[10] In sum, communities with a high proportion of single mothers have less economic power, less political power, and less social control than communities with a high proportion of two-parent families, and this affects all children in the community.

That said, we hasten to add that many single mothers are doing a heroic job of raising their children, and many children in single-parent families turn out very well. Indeed a society that had *no* divorce would not be desirable insofar as it would mean that women and children had no way of sustaining themselves on their own. A society that cares about children will always have a certain number of divorced and unmarried mothers. And it will protect and provide for these mothers, just as it protects and provides for widowed mothers. The issue is how large should this segment of the population be? In our opinion, 50 percent is too high a number.

## TABLE 14
### International comparisons of divorce rates, nonmarital births, and single parenthood.

| Country | Divorce rate | | Percent of all births to unmarried women | | Percent of families headed by single parents | |
|---|---|---|---|---|---|---|
| | 1960 | 1990 | 1960 | 1990 | 1960 | 1988 |
| United States | 9 | 21 | 5 | 28 | 9 | 23 |
| Canada | 2 | 12 | 4 | 24 | 9 | 15 |
| Denmark | 6 | 13 | 8 | 46 | 17 | 20 |
| France | 3 | 8 | 6 | 30 | 9 | 12 |
| Germany | 4 | 8 | 6 | 11 | 8 | 14 |
| Italy | 1 | 2 | 2 | 6 | NA | NA |
| The Netherlands | 2 | 8 | 1 | 11 | 9 | 15 |
| Sweden | 5 | 12 | 11 | 47 | 9 | 13 |
| United Kingdom | 2 | 12 | 5 | 28 | 6 | 13 |

*Sources:* U.S. Bureau of the Census, Statistical Abstract of the United States, 1993; Constance Sorrentino, "The Changing Family in International Perspective," *Monthly Labor Review,* March 1990, pp. 41–58.
*Note:* NA = Not available.

## ARE THE TRENDS IRREVERSIBLE?

Changes in children's living arrangements result from long-standing trends in marriage, divorce, and fertility. Divorce in the United States has increased since the turn of the century and has recently leveled off at a very high rate. Nonmarital birth rates have been going up gradually since at least the early 1940s. After 1960, the age at first marriage began to rise, increasing the proportion of young women "at risk" for becoming unwed mothers. Together, these forces have fueled the growth of single parenthood during the postwar period.[11]

These trends are occurring in all industrialized countries. Table 14 shows the increase in divorce rates, births to unmarried women, and single-parent families in nine industrialized countries. Divorce rates and births to unmarried women more than doubled in most countries between 1960 and 1990; in some places they increased fourfold. Single parenthood also increased in nearly all the countries between 1970 and the late 1980s. The United States has the highest prevalence of single-parent families, however, and it experienced the largest increase between 1970 and 1988.[12]

Some people have argued that the expansion of welfare benefits is responsible for the growth of single motherhood in the United States. They claim that welfare reduces the costs of single motherhood and discourages young parents from marrying. While it is true that in some parts of the country welfare offers poor women more economic security than marriage, the argument that welfare is responsible for the increase in single-parent families is flawed in several respects.[13]

First, the trend in welfare benefits between 1960 and 1990 does not match the trend in single motherhood very well. Both welfare benefits and single motherhood increased dramatically during the 1960s and early 1970s. After 1974, however, welfare benefits declined, while single motherhood continued to rise. The real value of the welfare benefit package (AFDC plus food stamps) for a family of four with no other income fell from $10,133 in 1972 to

$8,374 in 1980 and to $7,657 in 1992, a loss of 26 percent between 1972 and 1992.[14]

Second, increases in welfare cannot explain why single motherhood grew among women from higher socioeconomic backgrounds—women who are not likely to be motivated by the promise of a welfare benefit. Although women with a college education are less likely to divorce and less likely to become unwed mothers than women with a high school education (or less), they too experienced an increase in the risk of these events after 1960.

Third, welfare cannot explain why single motherhood is more common in the United States than in other industrialized countries. Nearly all the Western European countries have much more generous benefits for single mothers than the United States, and yet the prevalence of single motherhood is lower in these countries. The poverty rate for nonemployed single mothers is 69 percent in the United States, whereas it is around 28 percent in countries like Sweden, Denmark, France, The Netherlands, and the United Kingdom.[15]

If welfare is not causing the growth of single-mother families, what is? While no one can answer this question with certainty, we believe that three factors are primarily responsible for the changes in family structure that have occurred during the past three decades. The first is women's growing economic independence from men—women's ability to support themselves outside marriage.[16] Women who have their own source of income can be picky about when and whom they marry, they can leave bad marriages, and they can bear and raise children on their own, if they choose to do so. Thus we would expect to find more single mothers in a society in which women are more economically independent.

American women have been moving steadily toward economic independence throughout the twentieth century, in response to increases in the value of their time (hourly wage), greater control over fertility, and declines in the time required for housework. Since the turn of the century, each new cohort of young women has entered the labor force in greater proportions and has stayed at work longer than the previous cohort. By 1970 over half of all

American women were employed or looking for work, and by 1990 nearly three quarters were in the labor force.[17] While the rise in welfare benefits during the 1950s and 1960s may have made poor women less dependent on men by providing them with an alternative source of economic support, welfare was a small part of a much larger force that was making all women more independent.

A second factor contributing to the growth of single motherhood is the decline in men's earning power relative to women's. After World War II and up through the early 1970s, both men and women benefited from a strong economy and from the economic prosperity that swept the country. Thus, while women were becoming more self-sufficient during the 1950s and 1960s, men's wages and employment opportunities were increasing as well. Consequently, marriage continued to be economically rewarding, even though more and more women could afford to live alone. After 1970, however, the picture changed. The gender gap in earnings (women's earnings divided by men's earnings), which had been about 60 percent for as long as anyone could remember, began to narrow. In 1970 female workers earned 59 percent as much as male workers. In 1980 women earned 65 percent as much as men, and in 1990 they earned 74 percent as much as men. (These numbers apply to full-time workers between the ages of 25 and 34.) In just two short decades, the economic "gains" associated with marriage had declined by 15 percentage points. We would expect declines in the benefits of marriage to result in more single motherhood, especially when a substantial proportion of women are able to support themselves.

The narrowing of the wage gap occurred among all adults, but the experience was quite different for men and women from different socioeconomic backgrounds. For individuals with a college education, the wage gap narrowed because men and women were both doing well, but women were doing even better than men. Between 1980 and 1990 the earnings of college-educated women grew by 17 percent, while the earnings of college-educated men grew by only 5 percent (again, we are talking about the earnings of full-time workers, aged 25 to 34). Thus, while the benefits of marriage were declining, a woman still had much to gain from pooling resources with a man.

The story was much bleaker for individuals at the other end of the educational ladder. Between 1970 and 1990 women's earnings stagnated while men's earnings declined; women with a high school degree experienced a 2 percent decline in earnings, while men with a similar education experienced a 13 percent decline. The fact that less-skilled men experienced an absolute as well as a relative loss in earnings probably discouraged marriage even further since it indicated that many men were having trouble finding work and fulfilling the breadwinner role. Again, welfare may have played a part in making single motherhood more attractive than marriage for women with the least skills and education, but only because low-skilled men were having such a hard time and were receiving so little help from government.

Finally, changes in social norms and values during the 1960s also contributed to the growth of single motherhood by reducing the stigma associated with divorce and nonmarital childbearing and by making single motherhood a more acceptable alternative lifestyle. The revolution in sexual mores was especially important in this respect because it permitted young men and women to have intimate relationships and to live together outside marriage. In the 1950s, if a young unmarried woman found herself pregnant, the father of the child was expected to acknowledge his parenthood, and the couple were expected to get married. By the late 1980s expectations were very different, and unmarried couples were much less likely to resolve a pregnancy by getting married.

Attitudes about individual freedom versus the importance of the family also changed during the 1960s.[18] The new ideology encouraged people to put personal freedom and self-fulfillment above family commitments, and it also encouraged them to expect more from their marriages and to leave "bad" marriages if their expectations were not fulfilled. In the early 1960s over half of all women surveyed agreed with the statement "when there are children in the family, parents should stay together even if they don't get along."[19] By the 1980s only 20 percent held this view. Once sex and childrearing were "liberated" from marriage, and once women could support themselves on their own, two of the most important rationales for marriage were gone. Therefore, it is not surprising that when the economic gains to marriage declined in the 1970s, marriage rates declined as well.

The changes in social norms and values continue to influence family behavior by making new generations of young adults less trustful of the institution of marriage. Many of the young people who are having trouble finding and keeping a mate today are themselves the products of single-parent families. They were born during the 1960s when divorce rates were accelerating, and many of them have grown up in single-parent families or stepfamilies. Given their own experiences, these young people may find it difficult to make the "leap of faith" that is often the basis for making a long-term commitment. At the same time, their first-hand experience of single parenthood makes it easier for them to leave a bad relationship and to raise a child alone.

The changes described above provide a more complete explanation for the growth of single motherhood among different parts of the population at different times, as compared with the welfare argument, and they are consistent with cross-national differences. American women are more economically independent (and more individualistic) than women in most European countries, with the exception of the Scandinavian countries. For this reason alone we would expect to see more single-mother families in the United States than in countries like France, Germany, and Great Britain. More importantly, low-skilled men in the United States are worse off, relative to women, than low-skilled men in other countries. American workers were the first to experience the economic dislocations brought about by deindustrialization and economic restructuring. Throughout the 1970s, unemployment rates were higher in the United States than in most of the European countries, and wage rates fell more sharply here than elsewhere. During the 1980s unemployment spread to other countries, but with less dire consequences for men since unemployment benefits are more generous and coverage is more extensive in other countries than here.

Since these trends date far back in time and are occurring throughout industrialized Western countries, is there any reason to expect a reversal in family behavior? To the extent that single parenthood is caused by the increase in women's economic independence, the answer is no. The forces that are making women's wages go up—education, technological change—are not likely to be reversed, and if anything they will probably make women even more independent in the future. Nor are we likely to see an end to premarital and extramarital sexual relationships, although we could certainly do a better job of reducing the number of unwanted pregnancies among young people. To the extent that marital disruption and nonmarital childbearing are caused by a lack of support for poor fathers or poor two-parent families, however, and to the extent that they are caused by an overemphasis on individualistic values and a failure to enforce parental responsibility, it is possible that the trends in family behavior may level off or decline in the future.

## HOW CAN WE HELP CHILDREN?

The first step toward helping children in single-parent families is to make sure that parents understand the potential risks associated with divorce and nonmarital childbearing. Many parents are unaware that children who grow up with only one parent are more likely to have problems in school, to drop out of school prematurely, to become teen mothers, and to have trouble finding a steady job, as compared with children who grow up with both parents. Parents need to know that family disruption is associated with a higher risk of each of these negative events, and they need to know that their child is at risk regardless of their socioeconomic status. They also should realize that lack of income, and income loss associated with divorce, are responsible for about half of the disadvantages associated with living in a single-parent family, and that too little supervision and parental involvement and too much residential mobility account for most of the remaining disadvantage.

Many parents will be surprised to learn that children in stepfamilies do just as poorly, on average, as children in single-mother families. This rather startling finding underscores the fact that money is not the only deficit created by family disruption, and that remarriage is not necessarily a solution to single motherhood. While remarriage increases family income, it causes new strains and uncertainties within the family. It also leads to greater residential mobility, which often undermines children's connections to neighbors and friends.

Saying that we should do a better job of informing parents of the potential consequences of their decisions does not mean that we support the idea that divorce laws be made more restrictive. In our opinion, this policy will not strengthen families, and it might even have the opposite effect. Young adults in the United States—and elsewhere—are already delaying marriage and are instead entering into cohabiting relationships. Indeed, this is one reason for the increase in children born outside marriage. Similarly, remarriage has declined because divorced mothers are more likely to cohabit than they were in the past. Imposing additional costs on marriage will only make marriage less attractive, relative to cohabitation, and therefore people will marry less often. This, in turn, will undermine family commitments and make it even more difficult to enforce parental responsibility.

## HELPING TWO-PARENT FAMILIES

In addition to informing parents of the potential costs associated with family disruption, we believe that the government should be doing more to help two-parent families stay together. Certainly, we should make sure that parents who are married have the same support as parents who live apart.

Healthcare and childcare are two areas in which poor two-parent families receive less help from government than both well-off two-parent families and single-parent families. Nearly all middle-income and upper-income families receive medical insurance through their employers, and nearly all single-mother families are eligible for Medicaid. Poor two-parent families are the most likely to fall through the cracks in the healthcare system. If some variant of President

Clinton's proposal for universal healthcare coverage is adopted by Congress, this problem will be resolved. Similarly, middle-income and upper-income families can deduct childcare expenses from their income taxes, and single mothers on welfare are eligible for government-subsidized childcare. Poor and near-poor two-parent families receive virtually nothing in the way of government-subsidized help with childcare, because they pay no taxes. If we made the childcare tax credit a refundable credit, this would make the childcare benefit more equal across families.

We now have a very good program in the United States for subsidizing the earnings of low-wage workers with children: the Earned Income Tax Credit (EITC). This program matches each dollar earned with an additional benefit up to a specified limit. Starting in 1996, a two-parent family with two children and income below $28,000 will receive an additional 40 cents for every dollar earned up to a maximum of about $3,200 per year. These expansions in the EITC are a big step in the right direction, and they will do a great deal to reduce poverty and economic insecurity in two-parent families.

Unfortunately, the EITC is an earnings subsidy rather than an employment program. Thus, while it can increase the wages of a poor working parent, it cannot help that parent find a job. Unemployed parents in two-parent families are one of the most "underserved" groups in the United States. While, in principle, most workers are eligible for unemployment insurance, in practice only about half of unemployed workers are receiving benefits at any point in time.[20] Similarly, while in principle two-parent families are eligible for welfare, in practice very few qualify because the conditions for receiving welfare are more restrictive than those for single-parent families.[21]

If we are serious about supporting poor two-parent families, we must guarantee a job to all parents who are willing to work, both mothers and fathers. If each parent worked 30 hours a week and earned $5.00 an hour, the family income would be over $14,000 per year, which is just above the poverty line for a family of four. We could then limit the EITC to jobs that are not guaranteed by the government, so that parents would have a strong incentive to find their own jobs. The same two parents, working the same number of hours for the same wages in a nongovernment-guaranteed job, would have a family income of $20,000 if both received the EITC.

Finally, the United States is the only Western industrialized country that does not have a child allowance.[22] Instead, we have a child deduction that is worth quite a bit to middle-income families and worth nothing to poor families. To redress this inequity, and to provide more help to poor two-parent families, we recommend that the child deduction in the income tax be replaced with a child allowance worth $500 per child for all families.

## HELPING SINGLE PARENTS

Besides making sure that our policies do not discriminate against poor or near-poor two-parent families, we must do more to help single-parent families. While many people complain about the high cost of welfare, we actually do much less for single mothers than do other Western countries. And while single mothers rank near the bottom in terms of economic well-being in all countries, they are worse off in the United States than in most other countries.

The poverty rates are lower for single mothers who are in the labor force, but the relative rankings are similar; single mothers in the United States are more likely to be poor than single mothers in other countries, regardless of whether they work. To improve the economic conditions of single mothers in this country, we must change our helping strategy from one that places most of the burden on mothers to one that places more responsibility on fathers and society.

## FATHERS' RESPONSIBILITY

We must send a strong message to all nonresident fathers (or mothers) that they are expected to share their income with their child, regardless of whether they live with the child. This means making sure that all children have a child support award (including children born outside marriage), making sure that awards are adequate and indexed to increases in fathers' income, and making sure that obligations are paid in a timely fashion. In the past we have relied on judicial discretion and parental goodwill to enforce child support obligations, and the consequences have been devastating for children.

Enforcing child support will not only increase the income of single mothers, it will send a strong message to men that if they father a child they incur a responsibility to that child for at least eighteen years. This should make fathers more reluctant to divorce, and it should make men more careful about engaging in unprotected sexual intercourse. It will also send a message to women that if they have a child, they are expected to share parental responsibility with the father of the child. If a woman doesn't think a man would make a good father, she should make sure that she does not become pregnant with his child. The responsibility of the nonresident father should be nonnegotiable. Parents can decide to end their relationship with one another, but they cannot decide to end their obligation to their child. In addition, nonresident parents should have certain rights of access to their children which cannot be curtailed or terminated, except in cases where the court decides that the relationship is harmful to the child.

The Child Support Enforcement Act of 1984 and the Family Support Act of 1988 represent major steps in strengthening the child support system. The Family Support Act requires states to establish paternity, to establish guidelines for setting initial awards, to update awards on a regular basis, and to automatically withhold child support obligations from the paychecks of nonresident parents. While some progress has been made in each of these areas, there are vast differences across the states in the extent to which the reforms are being implemented. For example, the paternity establishment rate for children born outside marriage ranges from a low of 5.5 percent in Arizona to a high of 67 percent in Georgia.[23]

Needless to say, a stricter child support system has its drawbacks. Many people question the wisdom of forcing nonresident fathers to pay child support. They argue that fathers often are abusive and violent, and that stricter child support enforcement may endanger mothers and children. While we agree that some fathers may react this way, we do not believe that very many men fall into this category. Nor do we think that a majority of children should be deprived of child support because a minority of fathers cause problems. Rather, we believe that strong steps should be taken to protect single mothers and children from abusive fathers, just as strong steps should be taken to protect married mothers and children from abuse. But no one would argue that we should outlaw marriage because some fathers are abusive.

Our current child support system, which is highly discretionary, may actually encourage parental conflict. Nearly every father who is paying support knows someone just like himself who is paying less, and every mother knows someone just like herself who is receiving more. We suspect that a new, more rational child support system might reduce parental conflict insofar as parents would have a better idea of what would be expected of them in the event of a divorce or separation, and they might feel that the system was more equitable. Of course, if postseparation parental conflict is just a continuation of the conflict that led to the separation in the first place, rationalizing the child support system is not likely to resolve the underlying parental problem. Rather, the fact that child support encourages contact between the parents means that parents will have more opportunities to express their anger and hostility.

The best evidence we have to date on how fathers would behave under a new child support system suggests that the net effect of stricter child support enforcement would be positive for children.[24] The economic advantages appear to outweigh whatever disadvantages arise from greater parental contact and conflict. While encouraging, our evidence is very preliminary, and much more research is needed before we can be sure that the gains from stricter enforcement outweigh the potential costs.

Other people object to enforcing child support not because they are worried that fathers will become abusive but because they see child support as overburdening poor fathers. To some extent they are correct, although the inability of fathers to pay child support has been greatly exaggerated in the past. According to recent estimates, if all nonresident fathers were required to pay 17 percent of their income for one child or 25 percent of their income for two children, child support receipt would go up by $35 billion. These numbers take into account the fact that some fathers have no income or very low income.[25]

While many fathers could afford to pay much more than they are currently paying, it is also true that some fathers do not pay child support because they do not have a job or because their wages are so low that they can barely cover their own expenses. To address this problem, nonresident parents—like resident parents—should be guaranteed a minimum wage job, and those who find a private sector job (or a public nonguaranteed job) should be eligible for the EITC, even if they are not living with their child. Such a system would increase fathers' ability to pay child support and would be less punitive toward poor fathers. This would require restructuring the current EITC so that it is attached to the individual rather than the household and so that both parents in a two-parent family are eligible for a subsidy if their earnings are very low. Otherwise, some poor parents might decide to live apart in order to receive a second benefit. One way of accomplishing this would be to divide the existing benefit between the two parents and the child (or children). Each parent would receive a benefit irrespective of their residential status, and the parent living with the child would receive the child benefit as well as the adult benefit.

## MOTHERS' RESPONSIBILITY

The resident parent should be responsible for raising the child and for contributing economic support to the child. Most single mothers are doing this already. Over 70 percent are working at least part of the year, and over 25 percent are working full-time, year round.[26] These numbers are virtually identical to those for married mothers. While most single mothers are employed, a substantial minority depend entirely on welfare for their economic support. And some remain on welfare for as long as eighteen or twenty years. The Family Support Act of 1988 contains provisions that require mothers on welfare to seek employment outside the home, and many of the current proposals for welfare reform push even further in this direction, including putting time limits on welfare benefits. We agree with the general thrust of most of these proposals, at least in principle. We believe that in the long run, employment offers single mothers a better future than a life on welfare. Most married mothers prefer to work outside the home, and there is no reason to think that single mothers are any different. Ultimately, employment should increase a mother's earning power, as well as her self-esteem. And having a mother who is attached to the labor force should also be an advantage for a child when it comes to finding a job and planning for her own future.

Our major concern about the new proposals is that they reduce the amount of time mothers spend with their children. The loss of parental time could mean less parental involvement and supervision, which is harmful to children. Or it could lead to higher quality time spent with them and to more adult supervision, if the children were placed in good daycare and afterschool programs. The end result will depend a great deal on how many hours the mother works, the quality of the substitute care she has available, and the net income of the family, after deducting for childcare and other work-related expenses. If a child has less time with the mother and the family has no more income, he is likely to be worse off under the new system. If he has less time with the mother but good childcare and more income, he is likely to be better off.

The outcome of healthcare reform is another critical factor in determining whether single mothers and their children will be better off working than on welfare. If entering the labor force means losing Medicaid, this would be a serious setback for single-mother families. Establishing universal healthcare is a necessary if not sufficient condition for getting poor single mothers off welfare and into the labor force.

## GOVERNMENT'S RESPONSIBILITY

Government also has a responsibility to make sure that the basic needs of children in single-parent families are met. In addition to the programs described above—guaranteed jobs for fathers and for mothers, EITC for low-wage parents, a refundable childcare tax credit, a child allowance, and universal healthcare—the government should be responsible for collecting child support obligations. The Department of Internal Revenue does a good job of collecting income taxes and social security taxes, and there is no reason why a comparable arm of the government could not do just as good a job of collecting child support obligations.

In addition to enforcing private child support obligations, we believe that the government should provide all children with a guaranteed minimum child support benefit,[27] worth up to $2,000 per year for one child, to be paid by either the father or the government. Unlike welfare, a guaranteed child support benefit would not depend on mothers' income and therefore would not be reduced if the mother worked. Such a policy might encourage some couples to live apart in order to receive the $2,000 minimum benefit, but as long as the benefit was small, it would not have a large effect on living arrangements. Two parents living together would still be better off than two parents living apart because of economies of scale. Moreover, if we made nonresident parents eligible for the EITC, as discussed above, fathers could afford to pay more child support and fewer families would need the minimum benefit.

## NONMONETARY GOVERNMENT ACTION

While government is much better equipped to increase income than it is to increase other types of resources, local government could be doing much more to promote institutions outside the family and to build social capital for children. While this is an area in which we have no special expertise, we suspect that schools could play a pivotal role in building such institutions. Community service organizations such as those run by the Catholic, Jewish, and Lutheran social services agencies have provided this type of support in the past. Regardless of the provider, the key goal of such efforts should be (1) to reenforce parents' willingness and ability to foster their children's intellectual and moral development, and (2) to build links between children and other adults in the community who can serve as role models and sources of information as well as provide emotional support.

One way of achieving this goal would be to extend the school day and to use school facilities to provide extracurricular activities such as sports, arts, music education, and apprenticeships for older children and teenagers. Mentor programs that link children with adults, and internships that expose adolescents to the business community, are also good ideas for promoting the development of social capital.

Organizing children's afterschool time is clearly a major problem for many parents and one that requires a good deal of cooperation and coordination. At one time this valuable service was provided by nonemployed mothers, who spent much of their time planning children's activities and supervising children after school. The entry of these women into the labor force represents a major loss of resources for the community and for children, including those with nonemployed mothers. Nothing has replaced these resources during the past few decades, and children are increasingly left on their own to manage their afterschool hours.

Structuring children's afterschool time and providing adult supervision and mentoring would reduce children's opportunities for engaging in irresponsible behavior and would provide children with alternatives to the street gangs and "mall gangs" that are rapidly becoming the major organizers of youth activities in many communities. Structures such as these would also benefit children who are new in a community by facilitating friendships and fostering connections with adults other than their parents.

In addition to building community resources, we should give more consideration to promoting residential stability of children in single-parent families. Government has several levers for affecting whether or not parents move and how often they move. First, it can affect poor families directly through housing allowances and subsidies. Whatever is done to improve such housing and to increase residential stability will greatly benefit children in single-mother families, since they are the most likely to occupy this type of housing.

An excellent example of how public policy can enhance residential stability is an affordable housing project on Long Island where a number of single mothers were able to purchase homes in 1993. The mothers, who earned between $20,000 and $30,000 and who had not been able to get home mortgages in the past, became eligible for loans because banks relaxed their lending policies in response to 1989 federal legislation requiring commercial banks to report information on mortgages given to minorities and disadvantaged groups.[28]

The courts can encourage residential stability at the time of divorce. Property settlements could be arranged to allow children to remain in their current neighborhoods and schools for at least three years after the divorce, and judges could take the parents' willingness to stay in the same community into account in making custody decisions. In the latter case, decisions should be based on parents' willingness to remain in the same neighborhood rather than their economic ability to afford to do so. Otherwise such a policy would penalize mothers who have lower income than fathers after a divorce.

## SUMMING UP

The policy recommendations that we have outlined above are driven by three underlying principles. The first is that something must be done immediately to *reduce the economic insecurity* of children growing up in single-parent families. Low income or income loss is the single most important factor in accounting for the lower achievement of children in single-mother families. It accounts for half of the difference in educational achievement, weak labor force attachment, and early childbearing. Thus, raising income would go a long way toward closing the achievement gap between children in two-parent and single-parent families. The federal government has demonstrated considerable success in reducing the economic insecurity of the elderly, and there is no reason why the same cannot be done for children.

A second principle underlying our recommendations is *shared responsibility*. We believe the costs of raising children must be distributed more equally among men and women and between parents and nonparents. At present mothers are bearing a disproportionate share of the costs of children. Fairness demands that fathers and society at large assume greater responsibility. We also believe that shared responsibility extends to different levels of government—action by the federal government must be combined with responsibility at the local level. While the federal government can transfer income and collect child support obligations, it is not well equipped for fostering social capital in a community. This must be done by teachers, employers, religious leaders, and other community members who have a stake in the future of children.

The third, and perhaps most important, principle guiding our recommendations is that programs should be *universal*, that is, they should be available to all children and all parents. This emphasis underscores our belief that the problems facing single-parent families are not very different from the problems facing all parents. They are just more obvious and more pressing. While single mothers have the highest poverty rates of all families, many two-parent families have not done so well during the past two decades. And children in two-parent families have experienced a loss of parents' time as more and more mothers have entered the labor force.

Universal programs not only benefit a broader range of children, they avoid the dilemma of how to help children in one-parent families without increasing the prevalence of such families. In other words, they do not send a message to young men and women that they will receive help only if they live apart.

Finally, universal programs reenforce the idea that single motherhood is a risk shared not by a small subset of people but by the majority of the population. Growing up with a single parent is not something that happens to other people and other people's children; it is something that happens to us and to our children's children.

# Data
# and Variables

## THE DATA SETS

The evidence presented in this book is based on four nationally representative data sets: the Panel Study of Income Dynamics (PSID), the National Longitudinal Survey of Young Men and Women (NLSY), the High School and Beyond Study (HSB), and the National Survey of Families and Households (NSFH). Three of these surveys are longitudinal and follow people over time—the PSID, the NLSY, and the HSB. The fourth—NSFH—is a cross-sectional survey which asks people to recall their past experiences. (The NSFH is currently conducting a second wave of interviews with original sample members.) All four surveys provide information on family structure growing up and on children's well-being in young adulthood.

*The Panel Study of Income Dynamics.* The Panel Study of Income Dynamics is a nationally representative longitudinal survey of approximately 5,000 American families. The panel was started in 1968, and original panel members have been reinterviewed every year since then. The PSID oversampled poor families, which means that it overrepresents blacks and children living with single mothers. This is a very attractive feature of the data from our point of view, since it produces a relatively large number of single-parent families and black families. Children of original panel members are followed once they leave their parents' household, which means that we have information on their experiences during childhood and adulthood.

Most of the estimates from the PSID are based on a sample of children born between 1956 and 1965. These children were three to twelve years old when the panel was started in 1968, and they were in their mid-twenties to mid-thirties in the late 1980s. The sample contains about 2,900 individuals—1,475 white children, 1,300 black children, and 116 Hispanic children.

In parts of the analysis, we restrict the sample to children who were living with both parents at age twelve, and we use this sample to examine the effects of changes in family structure during adolescence on children's well-being. The *change sample* contains approximately 2,000 children.

The major strength of the PSID data is the information on family income during childhood. The Panel collects annual information on both family income and parents' marital status, which means that we can observe children's economic resources before and after their families break up. Information on total family income is collected directly from the household head and is generally regarded as quite accurate. Respondents were asked numerous questions about different sources of income, which increases the reliability of the income information.

Another unique feature of the PSID is the information on community resources. Questions about whether or not a family moved during the past year were asked every year, and these questions allow us to examine the relationship between residential mobility, family disruption, and child well-being. The PSID has recently appended census tract information to each household record, and this information can now be used to describe characteristics of the family's community, such as the percent of families in the census tract who are poor, percent of families who receive welfare, and percent of adult men not working.

The PSID is limited in a couple of respects. It does not contain information on parenting practices or parent-child relationships. Therefore, we cannot use these data in Chapter 6, which focuses on parenting variables. The lack of information on parenting is also unfortunate because it limits our ability to examine together the effects of income and parenting on child well-being. Ideally, we would like to know whether a loss of income associated with marital disruption is associated with a decline in the quality of parenting or whether the two types of losses are more or less independent from each other.

Another limitation of the PSID is that it suffers from a good deal of sample attrition. A large number of families dropped out of the panel between 1968 and 1969, and a small number continued to drop out in each of the next twenty years. Attrition can be a serious problem if the people who leave the sample are different from those who remain. In the case of the PSID, we suspect that attrition has affected our estimates of the effect of family disruption on idleness among young men.

*The National Longitudinal Survey of Young Men and Women.* The NLSY is a nationally representative sample of approximately 14,000 young men and women born between 1958 and 1965. Respondents were first interviewed in 1979 when they were between fourteen and twenty-one years of age, and they have been reinterviewed every year since 1979. The study was designed to provide information on the labor force behavior, education, and military service of a particular cohort. Thus it contains a broad array of young adult outcomes. Because we are interested in children's families prior to leaving home, we restrict the NLSY sample to respondents who were between the ages of fourteen and seventeen in 1979. Nearly all of these children were living with at least one parent at that age. The sample contains 5,246 young men and women, including 2,700 non-Hispanic whites, 1,521 blacks, and 780 Hispanics.

We also created a subsample of children who were living with both parents at the time of the initial survey in 1979 and who were between fourteen and fifteen years old. This is our *change sample*, and we used it to examine the effects of changes in family structure during adolescence on child well-being. Note that the age span covered by the NLSY data change sample (fourteen/fifteen to seventeen) is narrower than the age span covered by the PSID data (twelve to seventeen). This means that the NLSY sample contains fewer disruptions than the PSID sample. The sample contains 1,450 children.

The NLSY has a number of features that make it attractive for studying the effects of family disruption on child outcomes. It contains a large number of minority youth, including Hispanics as well as blacks. It has good information on child outcomes. And it provides some data on parental and community resources.

Unfortunately, the NLSY asks only one question about income while children are still living with their parents, and this increases the likelihood that income is measured with error. Once NLSY respondents establish their own households, the survey collects more detailed information on family income. But this information pertains to the income of the respondent as opposed to the income of the parents.

*The High School and Beyond Study.* The High School and Beyond Study is the third data set used in our study. Approximately 50,000 high school seniors and sophomores from 1,000 high schools in the United States were interviewed in 1980, and a subset of these students were reinterviewed in 1982, 1984, and 1986. Catholic schools and Hispanics were oversampled in the High School and Beyond Study. Because the HSB is a school-based sample, it only includes children who made it to the tenth grade. Early dropouts are missing from the survey. We limited our sample to students who were sophomores in 1980 and who participated in all four waves of data collection. This restriction yielded about 10,400 students, including 7,600 whites, 1,700 blacks, and 1,155 Hispanics. As before, we created a *change sample* that included all sophomores who were living with both parents in 1980. There were about 6,400 children in the change sample.

The primary aim of the HSB study was to collect information on school characteristics and students' curriculum and performance. These data are very rich with respect to information on school achievement and school-related behaviors. Another attractive feature of the data from our point of view is the information on parenting and parent-child relations. Information on parenting behavior was collected in both the sophomore and senior years. Thus for children whose parents separate between the two surveys we have data before and after the breakup. Note that the prior measures of parental resource necessarily are taken very near to the time of divorce and therefore are probably confounded with divorce. The HSB survey also contains information on community resources, including school characteristics and peer groups.

The primary limitation of the HSB survey is the lack of data on family income. The HSB study asked students about their parents' income, but this information is not very reliable. Much of it is missing, and there is considerable measurement error in that which exists. This is not surprising, since most sophomores do not know their parents' income. Another limitation of these data is the fact that children who dropped out of school or changed schools between the sophomore and senior years were not asked the same set of questions as those who stayed in the same school. This is true of a number of measures of parenting styles and peer quality used in this study.

*National Survey of Families and Households.* The National Survey of Families and Households is a nationally representative sample of adults carried out in 1987. Unlike the other data sets, the NSFH is a cross-sectional survey. Rather than following a set of individuals over time—from adolescence into adulthood—it collected information on family history retrospectively from a sample of adults. Respondents were asked to recall their family experiences growing up and to report about their past achievements (educational attainment, early marriage, early childbearing, and so on).

Information collected retrospectively is as good as information collected longitudinally so long as people are able to remember the events they are asked to describe. Most people in the population have no problem recalling whether they lived with one or both of their parents growing up. And most people are also able to accurately report their own marital and fertility histories and their own educational achievement. Answering questions about parent-child relationships growing up or about parents' income and community resources is more difficult.

Our analysis of the NSFH data is based on three samples. Our main sample (NSFH, Cohort 1) consists of men and women who were between the ages of twenty and thirty-four in 1987. These individuals were born close to the same time as respondents in the other three surveys: between 1953 and 1967. Our second sample (NSFH, Cohort 2) includes adults born between 1943 and 1952. We use these data to determine if the effects of family disruption on children have changed over time. Our third sample—NSFH, Parents—is a sample of adults who were raising children in 1987. We use these data to examine differences in parenting behavior across different types of families.

## THE VARIABLES

The analyses focus on three general areas of child well-being: educational attainment, idleness, and early family formation.

*Educational Attainment.* All of the surveys contain data on whether children completed high school, and most of them contain data on college enrollment and graduation. To measure high school graduation, we chose age twenty as our age limit. Thus, in our study, graduating from high school means getting a degree by age twenty. Three of the data sets—NLSY, HSB, and NSFH—allow us to distinguish between a high school diploma and a General Equivalency Diploma.

Three of the surveys include data on college enrollment and another three include data on college graduation. Enrollment is measured by age twenty, and college graduation is measured at the time of the last interview. The age limit for college graduation varies according to the data set we use. NLSY respondents were between twenty-four and thirty-one when we last observed them (1988); PSID respondents were between twenty-three and thirty-two, and NSFH respondents were between twenty and thirty-four. Our analysis of college attendance is based on children who completed high school, and our analysis of college graduation is based on children who enrolled in college.

The HSB study followed children through 1986, which means that most students (sophomores in 1980) had not had time to complete college when last interviewed. Thus, we only look at high school graduation and college enrollment with these data. The HSB provides information on school performance prior to high school graduation, however, and we use this to supplement our analyses of school achievement. Here we use students' grade-point average, attitude toward school, college aspirations, attendance, and test scores. These variables are described in more detail in Chapter 4.

*Idleness.* Idleness is defined as neither working nor being in school. In order to be classified as idle, respondents in the NLSY must have been inactive (at the time of the interview) for at least two years between the ages of nineteen and twenty-one. Students in the PSID and HSB samples were classified as idle if they were neither working nor in school at age twenty. We did not use the NSFH survey to examine idleness, since most of the respondents were beyond early adulthood and we were concerned about the reliability of the retrospective data. We also used the NLSY data to examine idleness in 1988.

*Family Formation.* Several indicators of early childbearing and family formation are examined, including teen marriage without children, teen marriage with children, and teen childbearing outside marriage. All four data sets provide information on early marriage and fertility. In addition, the HSB survey provides data on students' attitudes about premarital pregnancy.

*Family Structure.* Family structure is measured in several ways. In Chapter 4, we distinguish between children in *two-parent and one-parent* families. All children who had experienced a family disruption by age sixteen (including children born to unmarried parents) were coded as living in a one-parent family. In the PSID and NSFH, family structure is measured as of age sixteen. In the NLSY, it is measured in 1979 when children are between fourteen and seventeen. In the HSB, it is measured when respondents were sophomores in high school.

In Chapter 4 we examine different characteristics of children who were living in one-parent families at age sixteen. We look at the cause of the first disruption, the age of the child at the first disruption, the number of years spent with a single parent, the total number of disruptions, whether the mother remarried, and whether a grandmother lived in the household when the child was a teenager. This information is not available in all of the surveys, and therefore we rely primarily on the NSFH data for our estimates. We supplement the NSFH results with data from other surveys where possible. We also rely on the work of our colleague, Roger Wojtkiewicz, who has examined these issues in great detail.

In Chapters 5 through 7 we distinguish among children living in two-parent families, children living with single parents, and children living in stepfamilies. We also construct a variable that measures *change* in family structure. In the PSID, we look at changes that occur between ages twelve and seventeen. In the NLSY, we identify changes that occur between ages fourteen/fifteen and seventeen, and in the HSB we examine changes between the sophomore and senior years.

*Family Resources.* All of the surveys have some information on *family income* during adolescence. The PSID also has data on home and car ownership. The information on economic resources is described in more detail in Chapter 5, which examines the importance of income in accounting for differences in children's well-being.

The HSB has very good information on parental resources, including parents' involvement in school and supervision. This information is collected in both the sophomore and senior years. The NSFH (parent sample) has information on parents' activities with children, the extent to which parents praise or criticize their child, and the extent to which parents discipline their child. The NLSY asks two questions about parental involvement: whether the child has a significant adult in his or her life and whether that adult expects the child to go to college. These measures are described in more detail in Chapter 6, which examines the importance of parental resources in accounting for differences in child outcomes.

Finally, community resources are measured in several ways. The PSID has data on census tract characteristics, the NLSY has data on school quality, and the HSB has information on school quality and peer characteristics. Again, each of these measures is described in more detail in Chapter 7.

Three data sets have information on residential mobility. The PSID includes information on the total number of moves since the child was age twelve. The HSB records the number of moves during the school year since the fifth grade. And the NLSY has information on residential mobility between 1979 and 1983.

Other family background variables used in the analyses include race, parents' education, place of residence (region), sex of respondent, and number of siblings. Most of these variables are measured when the child was in his or her early teens. The means (proportions) for each of these variables are reported in Table A1.

## TABLE A1
### Means and proportions for dependent and independent variables.

| Variables | NLSY | HSB | PSID | NSFH1 | NSFH2 |
|---|---|---|---|---|---|
| **Outcome variables** | | | | | |
| Hsgrad | .20 | .11 | .18 | .11 | .10 |
| Diploma | .25 | .16 | NA | .20 | .17 |
| College attendance | .57 | .55 | .50 | .49 | .53 |
| College grad | .25 | NA | .42 | .19 | .30 |
| Idle | .18 | .15 | .26 | NA | NA |
| No marriage, no birth | .80 | .82 | .78 | .74 | .70 |
| Marriage, no birth | .08 | .07 | .09 | .11 | .14 |
| Marriage, birth | .06 | .05 | .08 | .08 | .12 |
| No marriage, birth | .07 | .05 | .05 | .07 | .04 |
| | | | | | |
| **Predictor variables** | | | | | |
| Two-parent families | .63 | .68 | .77 | .71 | .80 |
| Single-parent families | .19 | .17 | .16 | .14 | .09 |
| Stepfamilies | .07 | .11 | .07 | .10 | .07 |
| White | .75 | .80 | .82 | .81 | .86 |
| Black | .14 | .14 | .14 | .14 | .11 |
| Hispanic | .05 | .06 | .04 | .05 | .03 |
| Northeast | .21 | .21 | .24 | .20 | .20 |
| Northcentral | .31 | .29 | .28 | .28 | .27 |
| South | .32 | .34 | .29 | .33 | .34 |
| West | .16 | .15 | .20 | .19 | .19 |
| | | | | | |
| Mother's education | | | | | |
| (<hs) | .30 | .16 | .34 | .23 | .30 |
| (hs) | .50 | .56 | .49 | .52 | .51 |
| (>hs) | .20 | .29 | .17 | .25 | .19 |
| | | | | | |
| Father's education | | | | | |
| (<hs) | .28 | .17 | .32 | .24 | .35 |
| (hs) | .44 | .52 | .46 | .49 | .44 |
| (>hs) | .28 | .31 | .28 | .27 | .21 |
| | | | | | |
| Siblings (mean) | 3.21 | 2.84 | 3.65 | 2.98 | 3.06 |
| | | | | | |
| Total sample | 5248 | 10438 | 2919 | 4681 | 2474 |
| | | | | | |
| Change sample | 1450 | 6400 | 2000 | | |

# Bivariate Probit
# Models

---

The empirical analyses presented in this book are based on models which assume that the unobserved factors determining parents' decision to live separately and the unobserved factors determining child well-being (high school graduation, finding a job, delaying childbearing) do not covary with one another. If this assumption is violated—for example, if family disruption and child well-being are both caused by a third variable—our estimates of the effects of family disruption on children will be biased. An example of a variable that might be determining both family disruption and child well-being would be parental conflict. Another would be alcoholism. In both these instances, one might argue that high-conflict families (or alcoholic families) are more likely to break up and to have children who do poorly in school (or have other problems).

There are several statistical techniques for testing whether the unobservables affecting family disruption and child well-being are unrelated and for obtaining estimates of the "true" effect of family disruption, if the assumption of no association turns out to be wrong. All of these techniques require assumptions that are themselves open to question. Indeed, some people have argued that the cure to the problem of "unobserved differences" may be worse than the disease. Nevertheless, these techniques can provide us with useful information, and they can tell us whether the results based on simpler models are likely to be seriously misleading.

In a recent paper published in the *Journal of the American Statistical Association* 87 no. 417 (1992): 25–37 we used the NLSY data and a nonparametric statistical technique developed by Charles Manski to construct bounds on the effect of family disruption on high school graduation, making no assumptions about the joint determination of family structure and high school graduation. The results reported in that paper suggest that the estimates obtained from single-equation probit models, like the ones used in this book, fall within the nonparametric bounds. We have constructed similar bounds for the other two outcomes, using the NLSY, and for all the outcomes, using the PSID and HSB data. The results of these analyses are similar to those reported in the *JASA* paper.

In this appendix, we present results based on well-known parametric statistical techniques. To obtain estimates of the effect of living in a one-parent family, we use a bivariate probit model that treats both family disruption and child well-being as outcome variables. The equation predicting one-parent family status includes respondent's race (white, black, or Hispanic), mother's education (< twelve years, twelve years, thirteen years or more), father's education (same as mothers), whether mother has more education than father (Meduhi), and residential location (northeast, north-central, south, and west). The equation predicting child well-being includes race, mother's education, father's education, respondent's sex (in the high school graduation model), and whether or not the child's family is disrupted (disrupt).

In theory the same set of variables can be used in both equations, but in practice it is useful to have a variable or variables that affect family disruption but not children's outcomes. For this purpose, we use the difference in parents' education and residential location.

Table B1 reports results for the High School and Beyond sample. The first two columns report the coefficients and *t*-ratios for the model predicting high school graduation; the second two columns report the coefficients and *t* ratios for the model predicting teen birth; and the last two columns report the coefficients and *t* ratios for the model predicting idleness.

The constant and coefficients in the first eleven rows are from the equation predicting family disruption. Notice that the coefficient for mother having a higher education than father (Meduhi) is positive and statistically significant at the .05 level in the high school graduation and idleness equations but not in the teen birth equation. At least one of the three region coefficients is significant in each of the models. Living in the West has a positive effect on disruption in all three models, and living in the South has a positive effect in two of three models.

The constant and coefficients in the last ten rows are from the equations predicting high school graduation, teen childbearing, and idleness, respectively. The Rho coefficients, which are reported in the last row, tell us whether the unobservables or error terms for the equations predicting family disruption and child outcomes are correlated. In the high school graduation and idleness equations, the Rhos are not statistically significant; in the teen birth equation it is.

The family disruption coefficient, which is reported in the next to last row, is the variable we are most interested in. Notice that coming from a disrupted family has a negative effect on high school graduation and a positive effect on early childbearing and idleness. All of the coefficients are large and two are statistically significant. In sum, the bivariate equation models indicate that coming from a disrupted family reduces child well-being by a considerable amount, even after adjusting for unobserved differences.

Table B2 reports results for the NLSY data. The columns and rows are similar to those in Table B1. Meduhi is positively related to family disruption in the first two models, but not in the third. And living in the west is significant in all of the models, while living in the north-central region is significant in two.

In the NLSY data, the Rho is statistically significant in the high school graduation equation but not in the early childbearing or idleness equations. Family disruption is negatively related to high school graduation, and positively related to early childbearing and idleness, although the latter coefficient is not statistically significant.

Table B3 reports results for the PSID. Here the Meduhi coefficient is statistically significant in the high school graduation and idleness models but not in the teen childbearing model. The Rho is significant in the high school graduation and idleness equations but not in the early childbearing equation. In the high school graduation equation, the sign of the family disruption coefficient is positive, suggesting that family disruption *increases* children's school achievement once unobserved variables are taken into account. This last finding is the only piece of evidence we have that the negative association between family disruption and child well-being might be due to a third omitted variable.

In sum, we believe the bivariate estimates presented here support the hypothesis that growing up in a disrupted family reduces child well-being. In some of the models there is no evidence of correlated errors between the two equations predicting one-parent family status and child well-being. In others, there is evidence of correlated errors, but in these models the negative effects of family instability persist, even after taking account of correlated errors, except in the PSID model predicting high school graduation. While the coefficients for one-parent family status are not always statistically significant, they are in the expected direction (with one exception), and they are similar to the estimates obtained from the single-equation models. Taken in conjunction with the nonparametric bounds, we conclude that the estimates based on the single-equation models can be viewed as good evidence that residing in a disrupted family during childhood has negative consequences for children.

### TABLE B1
### Bivariate probit estimates for HSB data.

|  | High school graduation | | Teen births (women) | | Idleness (men) | |
|---|---|---|---|---|---|---|
|  | Coefficients | T-ratio | Coefficients | T-ratio | Coefficients | T-ratio |
| Constant | −0.65636 | −12.055 | −0.692047 | −9.477 | −0.72280 | −8.642 |
| BLACK | 0.59298 | 11.240 | 0.48260 | 6.634 | 0.69401 | 9.101 |
| HISP | −0.90208E-01 | −1.666 | 0.81666E-01 | 0.720 | −0.17199 | −1.617 |
| MEDU12 | −0.32689 | −6.762 | −0.25240 | −3.725 | −0.39381 | −5.692 |
| MEDU13 | −0.27668 | −4.663 | −0.18383 | −2.216 | −0.38520 | −4.530 |
| NFEDU12 | −0.10074 | −1.942 | −0.10288 | −1.504 | −0.50298E-01 | −0.637 |
| NFEDU13 | 0.48020E-01 | −0.761 | −0.11912 | −1.399 | 0.78813E-01 | 0.844 |
| MEDUHI | 0.12945 | 2.109 | 0.10041 | 1.196 | 0.21200 | 2.402 |
| NC | −0.14913E-01 | −0.314 | 0.16306E-01 | 0.252 | 0.17119E-01 | 0.249 |
| SO | 0.83614E-01 | 1.805 | 0.19776 | 3.175 | 0.32395E-01 | 0.475 |
| WE | 0.27420 | 4.918 | 0.15832 | 1.998 | 0.38140 | 4.911 |
| Constant | 0.50980 | 3.848 | −0.96480 | −15.267 | −1.0438 | −8.457 |
| SEX | 0.24411 | 6.090 | NA | NA | NA | NA |
| BLACK | 0.59879E-01 | 0.6172 | −0.11034E-01 | −0.127 | 0.20680E-01 | 0.146 |
| HISP | −0.48838 | −6.537 | 0.15893 | 1.409 | 0.12311 | 1.037 |
| MEDU12 | 0.38439 | 5.814 | −0.14749 | −2.341 | −0.15829 | −1.802 |
| MEDU13 | 0.37580 | 5.914 | −0.29788 | −4.225 | −0.13839 | −1.560 |
| NFEDU12 | 0.17008 | 3.200 | −0.79583E-01 | −1.228 | −0.87181E-01 | −1.180 |
| NFEDU13 | 0.43721 | 7.515 | −0.39642 | −5.538 | −0.48630 | −6.342 |
| DISRUPT | −0.84871 | −2.027 | 1.4977 | 6.905 | 0.64141 | 1.183 |
| Rho (1,2) | 0.26409 | 1.108 | −0.69996 | −6.346 | −0.29053 | −0.989 |

TABLE B2
**Bivariate probit estimates for NLSY data.**

| | High school graduation | | Teen birth (women) | | Idleness (men) | |
|---|---|---|---|---|---|---|
| | Coefficients | T-ratio | Coefficients | T-ratio | Coefficients | T-ratio |
| Constant | −0.53980 | −9.460 | −0.68729 | −8.182 | −0.42855 | −5.329 |
| BLACK | 0.79394 | 14.786 | 0.87442 | 11.478 | 0.73168 | 9.655 |
| HISP | 0.48065E-01 | 0.566 | 0.11809 | 0.988 | −0.56799E-02 | −0.047 |
| MEDU12 | −0.22886 | −3.447 | −0.20332 | −2.173 | −0.25985 | −2.687 |
| MEDU13 | −0.36329 | −3.938 | −0.38329 | −2.875 | −0.35777 | −2.746 |
| NFEDU12 | −0.90714E-01 | −1.431 | −0.87255E-03 | −0.010 | −0.16571 | −1.766 |
| NFEDU13 | −0.14935E-01 | −0.178 | −0.10414 | 0.865 | −0.10637 | −0.878 |
| MEDUHI | 0.21791 | 2.775 | 0.30477 | 2.724 | 0.14530 | 1.258 |
| NC | −0.14733 | −2.660 | −0.74086E-01 | −0.916 | −0.17291 | −2.189 |
| SO | −0.69922E-01 | −1.305 | −0.13073E-01 | −0.167 | −0.11267 | −1.472 |
| WE | 0.29171 | 4.750 | 0.32215 | 3.549 | 0.27290 | 3.153 |
| Constant | 0.59818 | 6.538 | −0.79322 | −7.023 | −0.97954 | −6.201 |
| SEX | 0.17788 | 4.360 | NA | NA | NA | NA |
| BLACK | 0.23260 | 2.382 | 0.21907 | 1.228 | 0.32028 | 1.952 |
| HISP | −0.17359 | −2.033 | 0.24749 | 1.984 | 0.92058E-01 | 0.674 |
| MEDU12 | 0.31829 | 5.849 | −0.41274 | −5.739 | −0.15905 | −1.928 |
| MEDU13 | 0.44493 | 5.854 | −0.88161 | −7.075 | −0.38807 | −3.435 |
| NFEDU12 | 0.28104 | 4.666 | 0.74175E-01 | −0.969 | −0.17417 | −1.947 |
| NFEDU13 | 0.38618 | 5.667 | −0.28846 | −2.878 | −0.25191 | −2.556 |
| DISRUPT | −1.0122 | −3.402 | 0.88121 | 1.948 | 0.41851 | 0.796 |
| Rho (1,2) | 0.33968 | 1.882 | −0.31048 | −1.156 | −0.16251 | −0.528 |

### TABLE B3
**Bivariate probit estimates for PSID data.**

| | High school graduation | | Teen birth (women) | | Idleness (men) | |
|---|---|---|---|---|---|---|
| | Coefficients | T-ratio | Coefficients | T-ratio | Coefficients | T-ratio |
| Constant | −0.56547 | −7.936 | −0.70976 | −7.017 | −0.37275 | −3.185 |
| BLACK | 0.65745 | 8.429 | 0.72771 | 7.014 | 0.59364 | 4.570 |
| HISP | −0.66312E-01 | −0.518 | 0.18051 | 1.108 | −0.36771 | −1.594 |
| MEDU12 | −0.37802 | −3.893 | −0.28895 | −2.044 | −0.44638 | −2.940 |
| MEDU13 | −0.33470 | −2.480 | −0.16713 | −0.846 | −0.48265 | −2.255 |
| NFEDU12 | −0.28052 | −3.176 | −0.33150 | −2.599 | −0.19414 | −1.493 |
| NFEDU13 | −0.31144E-01 | −0.262 | −0.19234 | −1.098 | 0.12938 | 0.702 |
| MEDUHI | 0.19162 | 1.777 | 0.25854E-01 | 0.157 | 0.27952 | 1.632 |
| NC | −0.98345E-03 | −0.014 | 0.24131 | 2.202 | −0.25027 | −2.107 |
| SO | −0.10856 | −1.552 | 0.97715E-01 | 0.919 | −0.33643 | −2.898 |
| WE | 0.19336 | 2.552 | 0.31462 | 2.709 | 0.19434E-01 | 0.161 |
| Constant | 0.14773 | 0.995 | −0.68391 | −2.567 | −0.71237 | −6.667 |
| SEX | 0.15675 | 2.862 | NA | NA | NA | NA |
| BLACK | −0.28558 | −2.336 | 0.18671 | 0.693 | 0.53829E-01 | 0.362 |
| HISP | −0.35567 | −2.815 | 0.77854 | 4.263 | 0.23011 | 1.151 |
| MEDU12 | 0.32801 | 4.838 | −0.36897 | −3.096 | −0.34322 | −3.201 |
| MEDU13 | 0.39270 | 3.719 | −1.0960 | −4.568 | −0.38398 | −2.444 |
| NFEDU12 | 0.38407 | 5.184 | −0.31863 | −2.194 | −0.17144 | −1.498 |
| NFEDU13 | 0.34635 | 4.153 | −0.39037 | −2.711 | −0.30183 | −2.363 |
| DISRUPT | 0.91201 | 2.687 | 0.63803 | 0.692 | 1.4781 | 5.003 |
| Rho (1,2) | −0.70827 | −3.231 | −0.69892E-01 | −0.129 | −0.68779 | −4.121 |

# Sex Differences

TABLE C1
**Teen marriage among women.**

| Family type | NLSY | PSID | HSB | NSFH1 | NSFH2 |
|---|---|---|---|---|---|
| Two-parent families | 12 | 12 | **9** | 15 | 17 |
| One-parent families | 12 | 13 | **12** | 12 | 17 |

*Sources:* National Longitudinal Survey of Youth, Panel Study of Income Dynamics, High School and Beyond Study, National Survey of Families and Households (1 = Cohort 1; 2 = Cohort 2).

*Note:* One-parent families include stepfamilies. All numbers are adjusted for race, mother's education, father's education, number of siblings, and place of residence. Statistically significant differences from two-parent families are in bold type.

### TABLE C2
### Family formation among men.

| Family formation and family type | NLSY | PSID | HSB | NSFH1 |
|---|---|---|---|---|
| **Teen marital birth** | | | | |
| Two-parent families | 2 | 3 | 3 | 4 |
| One-parent families | **3** | **7** | 2 | 4 |
| **Teen nonmarital birth** | | | | |
| Two-parent families | 3 | 1 | 2 | 2 |
| One-parent families | **5** | **6** | 2 | **5** |
| **Teen marriage** | | | | |
| Two-parent families | 4 | 6 | 4 | 6 |
| One-parent families | 5 | 6 | 5 | 6 |

*Sources:* National Longitudinal Survey of Youth, Panel Study of Income Dynamics, High School and Beyond Study, National Survey of Families and Households, Cohort 1.

*Note:* One-parent families include stepfamilies. All numbers are adjusted for race, mother's education, father's education, number of siblings, and place of residence. Statistically significant differences from two-parent families are in bold type.

### TABLE C3
### Sex differences in the effect of family disruption on dropping out of high school.

| Sex and family type | NLSY | PSID | HSB | NSFH |
|---|---|---|---|---|
| **Males** | | | | |
| Two-parent families | 14 | 17 | 6 | 6 |
| One-parent families | **29** | **24** | 14 | 12 |
| **Females** | | | | |
| Two-parent families | 9 | 11 | 5 | 7 |
| One-parent families | **27** | **22** | 11 | 13 |

*Sources:* National Survey of Families and Household (Cohort 1), High School and Beyond Study (Sophomore Cohort), Panel Study of Income Dynamics, and National Longitudinal Survey of Youth.

*Note:* Results are based on logistic regression models. All numbers are adjusted for race, mother's education, father's education, number of siblings, and place of residence. Statistically significant differences between males and females are in bold type.

# Notes

## 1. WHY WE CARE ABOUT SINGLE PARENTHOOD

1. For examples of the debate within the popular press, see op-ed by D. Popenoe, "The Controversial Truth: Two-Parent Families Are Better," *New York Times,* December 26, 1992, p. 21, and "Letters to the Editor," January 16, 1993, p. 21; see also B. D. Whitehead, "Dan Quayle Was Right," *Atlantic Monthly,* April 1993, pp. 47–84, and "Letters to the Editor," *Atlantic Monthly*, July 1993, pp. 8–11. For examples of the debate in the scholarly journals, see exchange among D. Popenoe, N. Glenn, J. Stacey, and P. Cowan in *Journal of Marriage and the Family* 55, no. 3 (1993): 527–556; P. Amato, L. Kurdeck, D. Demo, and K. Allen, *Journal of Marriage and the Family* 55, no. 1 (1993): 23–38.

2. Authors' estimates, based on the National Longitudinal Survey, 1979.

3. Larry Bumpass and Kelly Raley, "Trends in the Duration of Single-Parent Families, NSFH Working Paper No. 58, University of Wisconsin-Madison; Larry Bumpass, "Children and Marital Disruption: A Replication and Update," *Demography* 21 (1984): 71–82.

4. James Coleman, "Social Capital and the Creation of Human Capital," *American Journal of Sociology* 94 (1988): S95–S120. See also James Coleman, *Foundations of Social Theory* (Cambridge: Harvard University Press, 1990).

5. Larry Bumpass and James Sweet, "Children's Experience in Single-Parent Families: Implications of Cohabitation and Marital Transitions,"

*Family Planning Perspectives* 21, no. 6 (November/December 1989): 256–260.

6. Frank F. Furstenberg Jr., S. Philip Morgan, and Paul D. Allison, "Paternal Participation and Children's Well-Being," *American Sociological Review* 52 (1987): 695–701. Valarie King, "Nonresident Father Involvement and Child Well-being: Can Dads Make a Difference?" *Journal of Family Issues* 15, 1 (March 1994): 78–96.

7. Daniel P. Moynihan, *The Negro Family: The Case for National Action* (Washington, D.C.: Office of Planning and Research, United States Department of Labor, March 1965).

8. William Ryan, *Blaming the Victim* (New York: Vintage Books, 1971). For a discussion of the Moynihan controversy, see Lee Rainwater and William L. Yancey, *The Moynihan Report and the Politics of Controversy* (Cambridge: MIT Press, 1967).

9. See Russell Niele, "The Disintegration of the Black Lower Class Family: Charles Murray and William Julius Wilson on the Growth of the Ghetto Underclass," *Political Science Reviewer,* 20 (Spring 1991): 44–100, for a more detailed discussion of these issues and how they relate to the debate over the "culture of poverty."

10. These estimates are taken from the National Longitudinal Survey. See Appendix A.

11. Robert Emery, "Interparental Conflict and the Children of Discord and Divorce," *Psychological Bulletin* 92 (1982): 310–330.

12. For a discussion of the potential bias due to the use of nonexperimental data, see Andrew J. Cherlin, Frank F. Furstenberg Jr., P. Lindsay Chase-Lansdale, Kathleen E. Kiernan, Philip K. Robins, Donna Ruane Morrison, and Julien O. Teitler, "Longitudinal Studies of Effects of Divorce on Children in Great Britain and the United States," *Science* 252 (1991): 1386–1389.

13. We do not include religion or parents' occupation among our set of background characteristics because this information is not available in all the data sets and because, as shown in the example above, it does not alter the family structure effect once the other variables are taken into account.

14. Adjusting for predivorce well-being reduces the possibility that family instability is serving as a proxy for another variable, but it does not eliminate the problem altogether. A third unmeasured variable could be causing both a change in family structure and a change in children's well-being.

15. Also see Charles Manski, Gary D. Sandefur, Sara McLanahan, and Daniel Powers, "Alternative Estimates of the Effect of Family Structure during Adolescence on High School Graduation," *Journal of the American Statistical Association* 87, no. 417 (1992): 23–37.

16. Kenneth Auletta, *The Underclass* (New York: Random House, 1982).

17. Elizabeth Herzog and Cecilia E. Sudia, "Children in Fatherless Families," in B. Caldwell and H. N. Ricciuti, eds., *Review of Child Development Research*, vol. 3 (Chicago: University of Chicago Press, 1973), pp. 141–232.

18. Status attainment researchers, who used family structure in their models predicting socioeconomic attainment, found that coming from a "broken family" reduced educational attainment. See B. Duncan and O. D. Duncan, "Family Stability and Occupational Success," *Social Problems* 16 (1969): 273–283; O. D. Duncan, D. L. Featherman, and B. Duncan, *Socioeconomic Background and Achievement* (New York: Seminar Press, 1972); D. L. Featherman and R. M. Hauser, *Opportunity and Change* (New York: Academic Press, 1978); Christopher Jencks et al., *Inequality* (New York: Basic Books, 1972).

19. Carol Stack, *All Our Kin: Strategies for Survival in a Black Community* (New York: Harper and Row, 1974).

20. Judith S. Wallerstein and Joan B. Kelly, *Surviving the Breakup: How Children and Parents Cope with Divorce* (New York: Basic Books, 1980). E. Mavis Hetherington, Martha Cox, and Roger Cox, "The Aftermath of Divorce," in Joseph H. Stevens and Marilyn Mathews, eds., *Mother-Child, Father-Child Relations* (Washington, D.C.: National Association for the Education of Young Children Press, 1978), pp. 148–176.

21. See Frank F. Furstenberg Jr., Christine W. Nord, James L. Peterson, and Nicholas Zill, "The Life Course of Children of Divorce: Marital Disruption and Parental Contact," *American Sociological Review* 48 (October 1983): 656–668.

22. Judith S. Wallerstein and Sandra Blakeslee, *Second Chances: Women, Men, and Children a Decade after Divorce* (New York: Ticknor and Fields, 1989).

23. Bumpass and Sweet, "Children's Experience in Single-Parent Families"; Bumpass and Raley, "Trends in the Duration of Single-Parent Families."

24. Frank Furstenberg Jr. and Andrew Cherlin, *Divided Families* (Cambridge: Harvard University Press, 1991). For additional reviews of this

work, see E. M. Hetherington, K. A. Camara, and D. L. Featherman, "Achievement and Intellectual Functioning of Children in One Parent Households," in J. T. Spence, ed., *Achievement and Achievement Motives* (San Francisco: W. H. Freeman, 1983), pp. 205–284; Heather L. Ross and Isabel V. Sawhill, *Time of Transition: The Growth of Families Headed by Women* (Washington, D.C.: Urban Institute, 1975); Marybeth Shinn, "Father Absence and Children's Cognitive Development," *Psychological Bulletin* 85 (1978): 295–324; Irwin Garfinkel and Sara McLanahan, *Single Mothers and Their Children: A New American Dilemma* (Washington, D.C.: Urban Institute, 1986); Judith Seltzer, "Consequences of Marital Disruption for Children," *Annual Review of Sociology* 20 (1994): 235–266.

## 2. HOW FATHER ABSENCE LOWERS CHILDREN'S WELL-BEING

1. U.S. Census Bureau, *Statistical Abstract of the United States, 1991* (Washington, D.C.: U.S. Department of Commerce, 1992).

2. Stephen V. Cameron and James J. Heckman, "The Nonequivalence of High School Equivalents," *Journal of Labor Economics* 11, no. 1 (1993): 1–47.

3. Suzanne Bianchi, "The Changing Economic Roles of Women and Men," in *Changes and Challenges: America Moves toward 2000*, ed. R. Farley (New York: Russell Sage Foundation, forthcoming).

4. David Ellwood, "Teenage Unemployment: Permanent Scars or Temporary Blemishes?" in R. B. Freeman and D. A. Wise, eds., *The Youth Labor Market Problem: Its Nature, Causes, and Consequences* (Chicago: University of Chicago Press, 1982). The empirical evidence for the relationship between idleness in young adulthood and long-term economic well-being is much weaker than the evidence for the link between schooling and future well-being. Nevertheless, there are good theoretical reasons for believing that idleness is problematic, and therefore we have chosen to include it among our measures of well-being.

5. Barbara S. Mench and Denise B. Kandel, "Dropping Out of High-School and Drug Involvement," *Sociology of Education* 61 (April 1988): 95–113.

6. These numbers were provided by Finis Welch, and are based on the Current Population Surveys. The idleness measure includes persons

who were unemployed. See also Finis Welch, "The Employment of Black Men," *Journal of Labor Economics* 8, no. 1 (1990): S26–S74, and personal communication.

7. Ibid.

8. For a discussion of the debate over the effects of teenage childbearing, see Cheryl Hayes, ed., *Risking the Future* (Washington, D.C.: National Academy Press, 1987); Saul Hoffman, E. Michael Foster, and Frank Furstenberg Jr., "Re-evaluating the Costs of Teenage Childbearing," *Demography* 30 (1993): 1–14; Arline Geronimus and Sanders Korenman, "The Socioeconomic Consequences of Teen Childbearing Reconsidered," *Quarterly Journal of Economics* 107 (1992): 1187–1214.

9. *Vital Statistics of the United States, 1990,* vol. 1, *Natality* (Washington, D.C.: National Center for Health Statistics, Department of Health and Human Services, 1991).

10. David Ellwood, *Poor Support* (New York: Basic Books, 1988).

11. Greg J. Duncan and Saul D. Hoffman, "Teenage Underclass Behavior and Subsequent Poverty: Have the Rules Changed?" in Christopher Jencks and Paul E. Peterson, eds., *The Urban Underclass* (Washington, D.C.: The Brookings Institution, 1991), pp. 155–174.

12. Julie DaVanzo and M. Omar Rahman, "American Families: Trends and Correlates," *Population Index* 59, no. 3 (1993): 350–386.

13. These ideas are based on psychological, economic, and sociological theories of child development. For a discussion of child development theory, see Urie Bronfenbrenner, "Ecology of the Family as a Context for Human Development: Research Perspectives," *Developmental Psychology* 22, no. 6 (1986): 723–742; for a discussion of household production theory, see Gary Becker, *A Treatise on the Family*, enlarged ed. (Cambridge: Harvard University Press, 1991); and for discussion of social capital theory and the importance of social control, see Coleman, *The Foundations of Social Theory,* and Travis Hershi, *Causes of Delinquency* (Berkeley: University of California Press, 1969).

14. These numbers are based on the poverty threshold determined by the U.S. Bureau of the Census. United States Bureau of the Census, "Poverty in the United States: 1992," *Current Population Reports,* series P-60, no. 188 (Washington, D.C.: U.S. Government Printing Office, 1993).

15. Poverty among white single mothers is more often "event-caused," according to Bane. Mary Jo Bane, "Household Composition and Poverty," in Danziger and Weinberg, eds., *Fighting Poverty: What Works and*

*What Doesn't* (Cambridge: Harvard University Press, 1986), pp. 209–231.

16. U.S. Bureau of the Census, "Poverty in the United States: 1992," p. xxi.

17. Larry Bumpass, James Sweet, and Andrew Cherlin, "The Role of Cohabitation in Declining Rates of Marriage," *Journal of Marriage and the Family* 53, no. 4 (1991): 913–927.

18. These numbers are based on the poverty threshold determined by the U.S. Bureau of the Census, "Poverty in the United States: 1992."

19. Greg J. Duncan and Saul D. Hoffman, "A Reconsideration of the Economic Consequences of Marital Disruption," *Demography* 22 (1985): 485–498.

20. Irwin Garfinkel, *Assuring Child Support* (New York: Russell Sage, 1992).

21. Becker, *A Treatise on the Family*.

22. Yorem Weiss and Robert Willis, "Children as Collective Goods and Divorce Settlements," *Journal of Labor Economics* 3 (1985): 268–292.

23. James Coleman, "Social Capital and the Creation of Human Capital." See also Coleman, *Foundations of Social Theory*.

24. Frank Furstenberg Jr., S. Philip Morgan, and Paul Allison, "Parental Participation and Children's Well-Being," *American Sociological Review* 52 (1987): 695–701; Judith Seltzer, Nora Cate Schaeffer, and Hong-Wen Charng, "Family Ties after Divorce: The Relationship between Visiting and Paying Child Support," *Journal of Marriage and the Family* 51 (1989): 1013–1031. Judith Wallerstein and Sandra Blakeslee, *Second Chances: Women, Men, and Children a Decade after Divorce* (New York: Ticknor and Fields, 1989).

25. Judith S. Wallerstein and Joan B. Kelly, *Surviving the Breakup: How Children and Parents Cope with Divorce* (New York: Basic Books, 1980).

26. Ibid.

27. Maris A. Vinovskis and P. Lindsay Chase-Lansdale, "Hasty Marriage or Hasty Conclusions?" Reply to Frank Furstenberg Jr., "Bringing Back the Shotgun Wedding," *Public Interest* 90 (Winter 1988): 128–132.

28. Vonnie C. McLoyd and Leon Wilson, "The Strain of Living Poor: Parenting, Social Support, and Child Mental Health," in Aletha C. Huston, ed., *Children in Poverty: Child Development and Public Policy* (New York: Cambridge University Press, 1991), pp. 105–135. Jane D. McLeod and Michael J. Shanahan, "Poverty, Parenting, and Children's Mental Health," *American Sociological Review* 58 (1993): 351–366. E.

Mavis Hetherington, Martha Cox, and Roger Cox, "The Aftermath of Divorce," in Joseph H. Stevens and Marilyn Mathews, eds., *Mother-Child, Father-Child Relations* (Washington, D.C.: National Association for the Education of Young Children Press, 1978), pp. 148–176.

29. Diana Baumrind, "Effects of Authoritative Parental Control on Child Behavior," *Child Development* 37 (1966): 887–907; Diana Baumrind, "An Exploratory Study of Socialization Effects on Black Children: Some Black-White Comparisons," *Child Development* 43 (1972): 261–267.

30. Steven Nock, "The Family and Hierarchy," *Journal of Marriage and the Family* 50 (1988): 957–966.

31. Coleman, in "Social Capital in the Creation of Human Capital," refers to this structure as a "closed system" and argues that it promotes social capital.

32. Robert Weiss, "Growing Up a Little Faster: The Experience of Growing Up in a Single-Parent Household," *Journal of Social Issues* 35 (1979): 97–111.

33. For more on stepparents, see E. M. Hetherington and W. G. Clingempeel, *Coping with Marital Transitions: A Family Systems Perspective,* Monographs of the Society for Research in Child Development (Chicago: University of Chicago Press, 1992). See also Cherlin for a discussion of the institutional weakness of stepparent families, in "Remarriage as an Incomplete Institution," *American Journal of Sociology* 84 (1978): 634–650.

34. S. G. Kellam, M. E. Ensminger, and R. J. Turner, "Family Structure and the Mental Health of Children," *Archives of General Psychiatry* 34 (1977): 1012–1022.

35. P. L. Chase-Lansdale, J. Brooks-Gunn, and E. S. Zamsky, "Young African-American Multigenerational Families in Poverty: Quality of Mothering and Grandmothering," *Child Development* (forthcoming). See also L. M. Casper and D. P. Hogan, "Family Networks in Prenatal and Postnatal Health," *Social Biology* 37, no. 1: 84–102. Nan Marie Astone and Mary L. Washington, "The Association between Grandparental Coresidence and Adolescent Childbearing" (unpublished manuscript, 1994).

36. For reviews of research on the relationship between parental conflict, divorce, and child well-being, see P. R. Amato, "Children's Adjustment to Divorce: Theories, Hypotheses, and Empirical Support," *Journal of Marriage and the Family* 55, no. 1 (February 1993); Robert E. Emery,

"Interparental Conflict and the Children of Discord and Divorce," *Psychological Bulletin* 92 (1982): 310–330; D. S. Shaw and R. E. Emery, "Parental Conflict and Other Correlates of the Adjustment of School-aged Children Whose Parents Have Separated," *Journal of Abnormal Child Psychology* 15 (1987): 269–281.

37. Thomas Hanson, "Family Structure, Parental Conflict, and Child Well-being," Ph.D. thesis, University of Wisconsin, 1993.

38. D. P. Hogan and E. M. Kitagawa, "The Impact of Social Status, Family Structure and Neighborhood on the Fertility of Black Adolescents," *American Journal of Sociology* 90 (1985): 825–855.

39. S. S. McLanahan, "Family Structure and Stress: A Longitudinal Comparison of Male and Female-Headed Families," *Journal of Marriage and the Family* 45 (May 1983): 347–357; Robert Haveman, Barbara Wolfe, and James Spaulding, "Childhood Events and Circumstances Influencing High School Completion," *Demography* 28 (1991). A. Speare Jr. and F. K. Goldsheider, "Effects of Marital Status Change on Residential Mobility," *Journal of Marriage and the Family* 49, no. 2 (1987): 455–464.

40. S. S. McLanahan, T. Adelberg, and N. Wedemeyer, "Network Structure, Social Support, and Psychological Wellbeing in the Single Parent Family," *Journal of Marriage and the Family* (August 1981): 601–612.

41. Barbara Heyns, "Schooling and Cognitive Development: Is There a Season for Learning?" *Child Development* 58 (1987): 1151–1160.

42. Reginald Clark, *Family Life and School Achievement: Why Poor Black Children Succeed or Fail* (Chicago: University of Chicago Press, 1983).

43. The communities in Sullivan's study also differ with respect to race/ethnicity, and therefore we cannot be sure that the difference in employment patterns is due to differences in job networks rather than differences in ethnicity. However, the findings are consistent with the argument that job networks are important in connecting young men to the labor force. Mercer Sullivan, "Absent Fathers in the Inner City," in William Julius Wilson, ed., *The Ghetto Underclass* (Newbury Park: Sage Publications, 1993), pp. 65–75.

44. For a theoretical discussion of how adolescent behavior is affected by the absence of parental and social control, see Travis Hirschi, "Family Structure and Crime," in B. Christensen, ed., *When Families Fail: The Social Costs* (Rockford, IL: University Press of America, 1991), pp. 43–66.

45. Arland Thornton and Donald Camburn, "The Influence of the Family on Premarital Sexual Attitudes and Behavior," *Journal of Marriage and the Family* 24: 323–340.

46. Elijah Anderson, "Sex Codes and Family Life among Poor Inner-City Youths," in W. J. Wilson, ed., *The Ghetto Underclass: Social Science Perspectives,* special issue of the *Annals of the American Academy of Political and Social Science,* January 1989, pp. 59–78.

## 3. WHICH OUTCOMES ARE
## MOST AFFECTED

1. Dropout statistics are for persons aged fifteen to twenty-one, from *Statistical Abstract of the United States, 1991,* ed. 111 (Washington, D.C.: U.S. Government Printing Office, 1992). GED statistics are from Stephen V. Cameron and James J. Heckman, "The Nonequivalence of High School Equivalents," *Journal of Labor Economics,* 11, no. 1 (1993): 1–47.

2. All of the estimates presented in Figure 1 and the other figures and tables are based on logistic regression models and are adjusted for race, sex of child, mother's education, father's education, place of residence, and number of siblings. All differences are statistically significant unless noted in the figures, tables, and text. For additional analysis of family structure and educational attainment based on these data see Sara S. McLanahan, "Family Structure and the Reproduction of Poverty," *American Journal of Sociology* 90 (January 1985): 873–901; Nan Marie Astone and Sara S. McLanahan, "Family Structure, Parental Practices, and High School Completion," *American Sociological Review* 56 (June 1991): 309–320; Gary D. Sandefur, Sara S. McLanahan, and Roger Wojtkiewicz, "The Effects of Parental Marital Status during Adolescence on High School Graduation," *Social Forces* 71 (1): 103–122.

3. The lower dropout rates in the NSFH data could also be due to the fact that individuals were asked retrospective questions about their school achievement, whereas in the other surveys they were followed from year to year. The longer recall period in the NSFH may have led to more reporting error.

4. S. V. Cameron and J. J. Heckman, "The Nonequivalence of High School Equivalents."

5. In some of our data sets the effect of mothers' education is somewhat larger than the effect of family disruption and in others it is somewhat smaller.

6. Test scores account for only 10 percent of the difference in graduation rates and school attendance. They explain 75 percent of the difference in college expectations and 40 percent of the difference in grade-point average, however.

7. We do not estimate college graduation for the HSB sample, since respondents had not had time to finish college by 1986, the last year they were observed.

8. For additional information on the effects of family disruption on children's future earnings, see Kenneth A. Couch and Dean R. Lillard, "Parent's Marital History and Intergenerational Transmission of Earnings and Income," Research Paper #93-16, New York State College of Human Ecology, Cornell University.

9. For additional analysis of family structure and family formation see Sara S. McLanahan, "Family Structure and Dependency: Early Transitions to Female Household Headship," *Demography* 25 (February 1988): 1–16; Sara S. McLanahan and Larry Bumpass, "Intergenerational Consequences of Family Disruption," *American Journal of Sociology* 93 (July 1988): 130–152.

10. Kathleen Kiernan, "The Impact of Family Disruption in Childhood on Transitions Made in Young Adult Life," *Population Studies* 46 (1992): 213–234. Arland Thornton, "Influence of the Marital History of Parents on the Marital and Cohabitational Experiences of Children," *American Journal of Sociology* 96, no. 4 (1991): 868–894.

11. Steven Ruggles, "The Origins of African-American Family Structure," *American Sociological Review*, 59, 1 (February 1994): 136–151. S. Philip Morgan, Antonio McDaniel, Andrew T. Miller, and Samuel H. Preston, "Racial Differences in Household Structure at the Turn of the Century," *American Journal of Sociology* 98 (1993): 798–828. Linda Gordon and Sara S. McLanahan, "Single Parenthood in 1990," *Journal of Family History* 16 (1991): 97–116.

12. Douglas S. Massey, "American Apartheid: Segregation and the Making of the Underclass," *American Journal of Sociology* 96, 2 (September 1990): 329–357. Joleen Krischenman and Kathryn M. Neckerman, "We'd Love to Hire Them, But . . . : The Meaning of Race for Employers," in Christopher Jencks and Paul E. Peterson, eds., *The Urban Underclass* (Washington, D.C.: The Brookings Institution, 1991), pp. 203–234.

## 4. WHAT HURTS AND WHAT HELPS

1. Irwin Garfinkel and Sara McLanahan, *Single Mothers and Their Children: A New American Dilemma* (Washington, D.C.: The Urban Institute, 1986), chapter 3; Robert Moffitt, "Incentive Effects of the U.S. Welfare System: A Review," *Journal of Economic Literature* 30 (1992): 1–61.

2. U.S. Bureau of the Census, "Marital Status and Living Arrangements:

March 1990," *Current Population Reports,* series P-20, no. 450 (Washington, D.C.: U.S. Government Printing Office, 1991).

3. U. S. General Accounting Office, "Poverty Trends, 1980–88: Changes in Family Composition and Income Sources among the Poor" (Washington, D.C.: U.S. Government Printing Office, 1992).

4. Roger A. Wojtkiewicz, "Simplicity and Complexity in the Effects of Parental Structure on High School Graduation," *Demography* 30, 4 (November 1993): 701–717.

5. Lawrence Wu and Brian Martinson, "Family Structure and the Risk of a Premarital Birth," *American Sociological Review* 58, 2 (April 1993): 210–232.

6. Larry Bumpass and James Sweet, "Children's Experience in Single-Parent Families: Implications of Cohabitation and Marital Transitions," *Family Planning Perspectives* 21, no. 6 (November/December 1989): 256–260.

7. Andrew J. Cherlin and Frank F. Furstenberg Jr., *The New American Grandparent: A Place in the Family, A Life Apart* (New York: Basic Books, 1986).

## 5. THE VALUE OF MONEY

1. U.S. Bureau of the Census, "Poverty in the United States: 1992," *Current Population Reports,* series P-60, no. 188 (Washington, D.C.: U.S. Government Printing Office, 1993), p. A-8.

2. Income at age twelve was based on previous year's income, and income at age seventeen was based on current year's income. By comparing income at two points in time, we can address the question of whether low income is a cause or a consequence of divorce.

3. Our measures of predivorce and postdivorce income were taken during the 1970s and early 1980s. For children who were twelve in 1968, the period covered is 1967 to 1973. For children who were twelve in 1976, the period is 1975 to 1981. As before, income has been transformed into 1992 dollars.

4. All of the children in our sample were living with at least one parent, and none had experienced a disruption during the past year.

## 6. THE ROLE OF PARENTING

1. To get an idea of the degree of turnover in household personnel in single-mother families, see Sandra Hofferth, "Updating Children's Lifecourse," *Journal of Marriage and the Family* 47 (1985): 93–115.

2. Judith Seltzer reports a higher percentage of "no contact" for children born to unmarried parents—39 percent—than we do, which is probably due to the fact that she uses parents' marital status at time of birth to classify children, whereas we use mother's current status. Unmarried mothers who *never* marry are a select subgroup of all unmarried mothers and are likely to have more contact with the fathers of their children than the average unmarried mother. J. A. Seltzer, N. C. Schaeffer, and H. Charng, "Family Ties after Divorce: The Relationship between Visiting and Paying Child Support," *Journal of Marriage and the Family* 51 (1989): 1013–1031.

3. Frank F. Furstenberg Jr., S. Philip Morgan, and Paul D. Allison, "Paternal Participation and Children's Well-Being," *American Sociological Review* 52 (1987): 695–701.

4. Paul Amato and Sandra Rezare, "Contact with Nonresident Parents, Interpersonal Conflict and Children's Behavior," paper presented at the annual meetings of the Midwest Sociological Society, Chicago, Illinois, 1993.

5. The estimates reported in Tables 8–10 are taken from a study by Elizabeth Thomson, Sara S. McLanahan, and Roberta Braun-Curtin, "Family Structure, Gender, and Parental Socialization," *Journal of Marriage and the Family* 54 (May 1992): 368–378.

6. Unpublished results based on analyses by Elizabeth Thomson and Sara McLanahan.

7. E. Mavis Hetherington, Martha Cox, and Roger Cox, "The Aftermath of Divorce," in Joseph H. Stevens and Marilyn Mathews, eds., *Mother-Child, Father-Child Relations* (Washington, D.C.: National Association for the Education of Young Children Press, 1978), pp. 148–176.

8. E. M. Hetherington, K. A. Camara, and D. L. Featherman, "Achievement and Intellectual Functioning of Children in One Parent Households," in J. T. Spence, ed., *Achievement and Achievement Motives* (San Francisco: W. H. Freeman, 1983), pp. 205–284.

9. Hetherington, Cox, and Cox, "The Aftermath of Divorce."

10. The estimates for high school dropout, idleness, and teen birth are based on logistic regression models that control for parental education, residence, race, family size, and sex. Cases with missing data on parenting behavior are assigned to the modal category, and a dummy variable for missing data is included in the equation. All of the family disruption effects are statistically significant.

11. For additional information on the other studies, see Nan Astone and

Sara McLanahan, "Family Structure and High School Completion," *American Sociological Review* 56 (1991): 309–320; Nan Astone and Sara McLanahan, "Family Structure, Residential Mobility, and Education: A Research Note" (unpublished, 1994). The Astone and McLanahan study controlled for family socioeconomic status and excluded cases with missing data. In the current analyses, we included cases with missing data, and we controlled for parents' education rather than SES. The latter includes income and consumption items such as magazines and books in the household. The Thomson et al. study uses parents' reports of parental practices and a different set of outcome variables. Elizabeth Thomson, Thomas L. Hanson, and Sara McLanahan, "Family Structure and Child Well-Being: Economic Resources vs. Parental Behaviors," *Social Forces* (forthcoming).

12. See V. C. McLloyd, "The Impact of Economic Hardship on Black Families and Children: Psychological Distress, Parenting, Socioemotional Development," *Child Development* 61 (1990): 311–346; G. J. Duncan, J. Brooks-Gunn, and P. Klebanov, "Economic Deprivation and Early-Childhood Development," *Child Development* (forthcoming).

## 7. THE COMMUNITY CONNECTION

1. Urie Bronfenbrenner, "Ecology of the Family as a Context for Human Development: Research Perspectives," *Developmental Psychology* 22, 6 (1986): 723–742.

2. For more information on these data, see Michael Foster and Sara McLanahan, "A Beginner's Guide to Measuring Neighborhood Effects" (unpublished paper).

3. Percent of families headed by single women is an indicator of social control. Communities with a high percentage of single mothers have more crime and delinquency than communities with fewer single mothers, controlling for other factors such as median income, joblessness, race, and so on. Robert J. Sampson, "Urban Black Violence: The Effect of Male Joblessness and Family Disruption," *American Journal of Sociology* 92 (September 1987): 348–382.

4. Erol R. Ricketts and Isabel V. Sawhill, "Defining and Measuring the Underclass," *Journal of Policy Analysis and Management* 7 (Winter 1988): 316–325.

5. Douglas S. Massey and Nancy Denton, *American Apartheid: Segregation and the Making of the Underclass* (Cambridge: Harvard University Press,

1993). Reynolds Farley and William Frey, "Changes in the Segregation of Whites from Blacks," *American Sociological Review* 59, 1 (February 1994): 23–45.

6. The very low percentage of families living in underclass areas is due to the fact that the Ricketts-Sawhill-Mincey indicator is very restrictive. If we had used a different measure, such as areas in which 40 percent of the residents are poor, we would have found a higher percentage of families living in such areas. Single-mother families, however, would still have been disproportionately located in underclass areas. See Sara McLanahan, Irwin Garfinkel, and Dorothy Watson, "Single Mothers, the Underclass, and Social Policy," in W. J. Wilson, ed., *The Ghetto Underclass: Social Science Perspectives,* special issue of *Annals of the American Academy of Political and Social Science* 501 (January 1989): 92–104.

7. William Julius Wilson, *The Truly Disadvantaged* (Chicago: University of Chicago Press, 1987).

8. See Massey and Denton, *American Apartheid: Segregation and the Making of the Underclass.*

9. Estimates are based on models that control for respondents' sex and race, parents' education, number of siblings, and region of residence. In the NLSY data, only the effect of single parenthood is statistically significant. In the HSB data, both the single-parent family and step-family effects are significant.

10. See also Alden Speare Jr. and Frances K. Goldscheider, "Effects of Marital Status Change on Residential Mobility," *Journal of Marriage and the Family* 49 (May 1987): 455–464; L. Long, "International Perspectives on the Residential Mobility of America's Children," *Journal of Marriage and the Family* 54, no. 4 (1992): 861–869.

11. Nan Astone and Sara McLanahan, "Family Structure, Residential Mobility, and Education: A Research Note" (unpublished, 1994). M. Anne Hill and June O'Neill, "Family Endowments and the Achievement of Young Children with Special Reference to the Underclass" (unpublished manuscript).

## 8. WHAT SHOULD BE DONE

1. Sara McLanahan and Julia Adams, "Parenthood and Psychological Well-Being," *Annual Review of Sociology* 13 (1987): 237–257.

2. Urie Bronfenbrenner argues that in order to carry out his or her childrearing task, the primary parent needs the support of a second

adult. While it is certainly not impossible for a single mother to have as much, or even more, support than a married mother, it is more difficult and less likely. See Urie Bronfenbrenner, "Ecology of the Family as a Context for Human Development: Research Perspectives," *Developmental Psychology* 22, no. 6 (1986): 723–742.

3. Men who live with children are spending somewhat more time in childcare, but fewer men overall are living with children. Arlie Hochschild, *The Second Shift* (New York: Viking Press, 1989); Frances Goldscheider and Linda Waite, *New Families, No Families?* (Berkeley: University of California Press, 1991).

4. Greg Duncan and Saul Hoffman, "A Reconsideration of the Economic Consequences of Divorce," *Demography* 22 (1985): 485–497. Karen Holden and Pamela Smock, "The Economic Costs of Marital Dissolution: Why Do Women Bear a Disproportionate Cost?" *Annual Review of Sociology* 17 (1991): 51–78.

5. Sanders Korenman and David Neumark, "Does Marriage Really Make Men More Productive?" *Journal of Human Resources* 26, no. 2 (1990): 282–307.

6. Walter Gove, "The Relationship between Sex Roles, Marital Status, and Mental Illness," *Social Forces* 51 (1972): 34–44.

7. Alice Rossi and Peter Rossi, *Of Human Bonding: Parent-Child Relations across the Life Course* (New York: A. de Gruyter, 1990); Debra Umberson, "Relationships between Adult Children and Their Parents: Psychological Consequences for Both Generations," *Journal of Marriage and the Family* 54 (August 1992): 664–674.

8. Samuel Preston, "Children and the Elderly: Divergent Paths for America's Dependents," *Demography* 21 (1984): 435–457.

9. S. Kellam, R. Adams, C. Brown, and M. Ensminger, "The Long-Term Evolution of the Family Structure of Teenage and Older Mothers," *Journal of Marriage and the Family* 44 (1982): 539–554; B. Bloom, "A Census Tract Analysis of Socially Deviant Behaviors," *Multivariate Behavioral Research* 1 (1966): 307–320. Cited in Robert J. Sampson, "Urban Black Violence: The Effect of Male Joblessness and Family Disruption," *American Journal of Sociology* 92 (September 1987): 348–382.

10. Sampson, "Urban Black Violence."

11. Sara McLanahan and Lynne Casper, "The American Family in 1990: Growing Diversity and Inequality," in *Changes and Challenges: America Moves toward 2000*, ed. R. Farley (New York: Russell Sage Foundation, forthcoming).

12. We should note that in Denmark and Sweden nonmarital fertility is even higher than it is in the United States. However, in these countries, the vast majority of unmarried parents are cohabiting and raising their child together. Constance Sorrentino, "The Changing Family in International Perspective," *Monthly Labor Review* (March 1990): 41–58.

13. See I. Garfinkel and S. S. McLanahan, *Single Mothers and Their Children: A New American Dilemma* (Washington, D.C.: Urban Institute, 1986). Robert Moffitt, "Incentive Effects of the U.S. Welfare System: A Review," *Journal of Economic Literature* 30 (1992): 1–61.

14. Committee on Ways and Means, U.S. House of Representatives, "Overview of Entitlement Programs" (Washington, D.C.: U.S. Government Printing Office, 1993).

15. Poverty is defined as adjusted family income less than 50 percent of the median adjusted family income. Sara McLanahan, Lynne Casper, and Annamette Sorensen, "Women's Roles and Women's Economic Status in Eight Industrialized Countries," in *Gender and Family Change in Industrialized Countries,* ed. K. O. Mason and S. M. Jensen (Oxford: Oxford University Press, forthcoming).

16. Barbara Bergman, *The Economic Emergence of Women* (New York: Basic Books, 1986).

17. In the following discussion of women's employment patterns and women's earnings, we rely on Suzanne Bianchi and Daphne Spain, *American Women in Transition* (New York: Russell Sage Foundation, 1986); Suzanne Bianchi, "The Changing Economic Roles of Women and Men," in *Changes and Challenges: America Moves toward 2000,* ed. R. Farley (New York: Russell Sage Foundation, forthcoming).

18. R. Lesthaeghe and J. Surkyn, "Cultural Dynamics and Economic Theories of Fertility Change," *Population and Development Review* 14 (1988): 1–45. R. Bellah, R. Adsen, A. Swindler, W. Sullivan, and S. Tipton, *Habits of the Heart: Individualism and Commitment in American Life* (Berkeley: University of California Press, 1985).

19. Arland Thornton, "Changing Attitudes toward Family Issues in the United States," *Journal of Marriage and the Family* 51 (1989): 873–895.

20. Committee on Ways and Means, "Overview of Entitlement Programs."

21. Two-parent families are eligible for AFDC-U in most states if they meet the income test, but very few two-parent families are poor enough to do so.

22. Sheila Kamerman and Alfred J. Kahn, "What Europe Does for Single Parent Families," *Public Interest* 93 (1988): 70–86.

23. Committee on Ways and Means, "Overview of Entitlement Programs."

24. Sara McLanahan, Judith Seltzer, Thomas Hanson, and Elizabeth Thomson, "Child Support Enforcement and Child Well-being: Greater Security or Greater Conflict?" in I. Garfinkel, S. S. McLanahan, and P. Robbins, eds., *Child Support and Child Wellbeing* (Washington, D.C.: Urban Institute Press, forthcoming).

25. Cynthia Miller, Irwin Garfinkel, and Sara McLanahan, "Fathers' Ability to Pay Child Support," paper presented at Conference on Reshaping the Family: Social and Economic Changes and Public Policy, sponsored by the RAND Population Center and the UCLA Economics Department, Los Angeles, California, January 1994.

26. Suzanne Bianchi, "The Changing Economic Roles of Women and Men," in *Changes and Challenges: America Moves toward 2000*, ed. R. Farley (New York: Russell Sage Foundation, forthcoming).

27. For more details on a minimum child support benefit, see Irwin Garfinkel, *Assuring Child Support* (New York: Russell Sage Foundation, 1992). See also National Commission on Children, *Beyond Rhetoric: A New American Agenda for Children and Families* (Washington, D.C.: U.S. Government Printing Office, 1991).

28. Peter Marks, *New York Times,* September 26, 1993, Metro Report, p. 1.

# Index